The National 9/11 Memorials

The National 9/11 Memorials

A Photographic Guide

Brian M. Holmes

and Min Xie

The National 9/11 Memorials – A Photographic Guide copyright ©2012, 2017 by Brian M. Holmes and Min Xie. All rights reserved. Printed in the United States of America. No part of this book may be used or reproduced in any manner without written permission except in the case of brief quotations as part of critical articles and reviews. For more information 911memorials@gmail.com, www.nj911memorials.com.

Holmes House Press

Second edition November 2017

Book Design by Brian M. Holmes

ISBN-13: 978-1979629058

ISBN-10: 1979629056

To all those who perished on September 11, 2001. You are remembered.

Contents

Preface 9

Acknowledgements 11

Introduction 13

The Story of 9/11 17

National 9/11 Memorial at the World Trade Center, New York City 27

The Pentagon 9/11 Memorial 45

Flight 93 National Memorial, Shanksville, Pennsylvania 66

Boston's Logan International Airport, Boston, Massachusetts 79

The Victims of September 11, 2001 91

Sources 109

Illustrations 110

INDEX 111

About the Authors 113

Preface

September 11, 2001 is a day that will be remembered in the United States for decades to come, if not forever. The day that America was attacked by terrorists and nearly 3,000 innocent citizens and foreign-born residents were murdered has been memorialized by the citizens of cities and towns all over the U.S., and indeed in many countries around the world.

This book of photography (and some history) focuses on just four important September 11 memorials –memorials of national importance because they are closely aligned with the events of that awful day. Unfortunately, many people may never get around to visiting all of the national memorials, and that's a shame because each is, in its own way, a fine work of art as well as a heartfelt remembrance of loved ones.

The National 9/11 Memorials – A Photographic Guide takes you on an up-close, and personal visit to the three memorials run by the federal government and another run by the Massachusetts Port Authority in Boston. The book brings to you, in one place, dozens of beautiful color photographs along with pertinent background information about each memorial. The photographs and information gathered in this book may inspire (hopefully) the reader to go out on his or her own journey to visit these moving memorials, or the reader may just appreciate them within the book's pages. In addition, *The National 9/11 Memorials* includes the historical background, timeline information concerning the terrorist attacks and the responses in the ensuing years, and a list of victims of the tragic day.

Never before has a book brought together so many photographs of these four September 11 memorials and information about them in one place so that the reader can participate in the honoring of the victims of the worst terrorist attack ever against the American people. It is humbly hoped that *The National 9/11 Memorials – A Photographic Guide* will spread awareness of these beautiful and heart-felt tributes and contribute to the everlasting preservation of remembrances of the lives of our lost brothers and sisters in the terrorist attacks of 2001. As the National September 11 Memorial and Museum in New York City states on a wall near the victims' remains, "No Day Shall Erase You from the Memory of Time". This is the object of every 9/11 memorial, and the object of *The National 9/11 Memorials – A Photographic Guide*.

Acknowledgements

Thank you to my wife Min Xie for her excellent photography and photo editing, and for her forbearance with my lack of employment throughout much of the production of this book. I am lucky to have found such a patient and loving wife who shares so many interests with me.

I would also like to thank the people around me, co-workers, friends and family, for encouraging me in my desire to see through this endeavor. Producing a book is a challenge, and sometimes, when the inevitable walls and closed doors present themselves, we all need a little reinvigoration of our drive.

I would also like to acknowledge Napoleon Hill, Angela Booth, and John Locke for their inspirational writing. These three writers motivated me over the course of this book's production.

Introduction

On the morning of September 11, 2001, I was on my way to work, as was the rest of the United States' east coast. The September sky in New Jersey was a brilliant blue with literally not a cloud in sight. The leaves were only just getting ready to change color and were still two or three weeks from falling. The summer humidity was gone and the temperature was seasonably warm for 8:45 in the morning. I was in my car driving alongside the Earle Naval Weapons Station on Route 34's long, straight, fenced-in stretch through that base. (The public highway bisects the naval base for three or four miles.)

I was listening to a New York City morning radio personality, someone who was always good for a laugh or two on the way to work. Not long after 8:47 a.m., his producer came on the air and said that an airplane had hit one of towers of the World Trade Center. The information was sketchy and the authorities and media weren't even sure what kind of plane it was (i.e., whether it was a small single engine plane or what). It was literally moments since it had happened. But the radio host was already speculating about Osama bin Laden being behind it, and so was I. I don't remember if I had made it to work before the second plane hit. But when that happened, there was no doubt in anyone's mind that this was no accident. I was stunned and so were my co-workers. To a great extent, that day changed every day which followed it for Americans and the world.

After the second passenger jet hit the South tower of the World Trade Center, the day was largely a wasted work day. People were looking for news reports on the Internet, streaming news reports, watching the events on the TV in the cafeteria, and listening to radios. There were quiet, shocked discussions amongst employees. Soon other planes hit the Pentagon, and a Pennsylvania field and speculation at work was running wild. Would this keep happening all day long? Then, after burning for more than an hour, the World Trade Center towers fell. For hours we were waiting for more planes to hit more targets. The airspace over the United States was shut down in an effort to prevent any more possible terrorist acts, and orders were given to shoot down any plane not following Federal Aviation Administration (FAA) instructions. President Bush appeared to be missing in action.

The Damaged Pentagon

On that morning, there was question as to whether United Flight 93, which went down in a Shanksville, Pennsylvania field, was shot down. We found out later in the day that it wasn't. Instead there was heroism on that plane. Heroism and sacrifice which cost the hero passengers of that flight their lives, but which may have saved hundreds of other lives, and prevented the destruction of yet another symbol of America, the White House or the United States Capitol building.

There were heroes on United Flight 93, and there were heroes at the World Trade Center in New York City and at The Pentagon in Washington D.C. And President Bush did arrive back in Washington D.C. later that day and in the evening spoke to a worried nation and the world about the terrible event.

Crash at Shanksville, PA

The 3000 people who died on September 11, 2001 and the heroes that saved lives that day have had memorials erected in their honor all over the United States of America. New York, New Jersey, Pennsylvania, Connecticut, Washington D.C., and more, are all host to hundreds of these tangible remembrances. But the memorials are also found in many additional states, and even in other countries. Some are made of granite, steel, or brass. Many incorporate trees and other living things into the memorial's design. Many are benches, or gardens, or memorial flagpoles. There is a wide range of creativity displayed in

The U.S. Capitol

all of these tributes. The one thing they all have in common is that they were conceived with reverence and love for innocent and/or brave fellow citizens and family members.

In the pages which follow, my co-photographer Min Xie and I present the four "national" September 11 memorials. The four "national" memorials are three of them run by the federal government (the World Trade Center memorial, The Pentagon memorial, and the Shanksville memorial) and one in Boston at Boston Logan airport (run by the Massachusetts Port Authority) which is included because of the fact that two of the hijacked planes took off from there.

The average person will only be able to see a handful of memorials in their everyday life. Perhaps at the train station or town square in their own town, or at a county park in a nearby town. In fact, getting out and seeing the memorial in your own town (if it has one) is something that everyone should do, especially on September 11 when there are usually special memorial services taking place. But one should also remember that the memorials placed in our town squares are there to be viewed at any time, and should be. It is one more thing which connects us to our communities, and fellow Americans.

The four memorials presented in this book are beautiful and reverent September 11 memorials and deserve wider appreciation, especially the three that aren't at Ground Zero, which has already garnered millions of visitors a year. Min and I wanted to see these ourselves and share them with you. That is the purpose of this book. To honor the lives of the heroes and victims of September 11 by giving their memorials a larger audience. *The National 9/11 Memorials – A Photographic Guide* allows you to see and appreciate memorials that you may never get to see for yourself in person. You can participate in the reverence, honor, and beauty of each 9/11 memorial without having to fly or drive miles to see it.

The National 9/11 Memorials starts out with beautiful, high resolution, color photographs of each national 9/11 memorial. This is accompanied by information such as what material it's made of, the memorial's designers, and the inscriptions on or

A Statement on the Pentagon 9/11 Memorial

near the monuments. The names of all of the people who died as a result of the tragedy that day are included in this book in the Victims of September 11, 2001 chapter.

September 11, 2001 is a tragic day that all Americans wish had never happened. We came together in shock and determination as a country that day, in a way that we rarely do. In May 2011, nearly ten years after the worst act of terrorism ever committed, Osama bin Ladin, the impetus behind the attacks and al Qaeda was finally brought to justice when U.S. forces tracked him down to his hideout in Pakistan and killed him. The U.S. and much of the world sighed with relief and joy that the recent embodiment of evil in the world had finally been dealt with. September 11 "mastermind" Khalid Sheik Mohammed's trial began only in May of 2012, even though he had been in custody since 2003.

Every day brings new attempts by al Qaeda and its supporters to kill vulnerable, innocent civilians <u>wherever</u> in the world they can. The fight begun more than ten years ago by al Qaeda goes on. Evil acts perpetrated on freedom-loving people continue on a daily basis. The U.S. and other governments continue to hound, hunt, capture, and/or kill al Qaeda and related terrorists all over the world. Unfortunately, there seems to be no decrease in the terrorists' efforts.

It is my hope that this book, *The National 9/11 Memorials – A Photographic Guide*, will be part of the national effort to always remember a day when the United States of America was attacked by evil people, and when the world realized that Osama bin Ladin and other Islamic extremists were engaged in a war against it, a war which must be fought until good people win over a cowardly, disillusioned, and evil ideology.

Please enjoy *The National 9/11 Memorials* and remember the heroes of that day. As the National September 11 Memorial and Museum states on a wall near the victims' remains,

"No Day Shall Erase You from the Memory of Time"

The Story of 9/11

Before 9/11

The story of 9/11 is not just the story of what happened on the day of September 11, 2001, although the events of that day are extremely important and have changed the way Americans interact with the world. The story of 9/11 is also rooted in the context of events which happened over the previous 25 or 30 years leading up to that terrible day. That history is long and complicated and not suited to a photographical book. Some of the important events are touched on here. For an in-depth background into the historical context leading up to 9/11 you can refer to *The 9/11 Commission Report*, which tells the story very well.

1978 The Soviet Union invades Afghanistan in an attempt to buttress a failing Marxist Afghan government against Islamic rebels.

1979 Iran's Shah, Mohammed Reza Pahlavi, is overthrown in an Islamic Revolution leading to the rule of a fundamentalist Islamic republic by the Ayatollah Ruhollah Khomeini.

1979 Iranian "students" storm the U.S. embassy in Tehran taking 66 people hostage in a hostage crisis that lasts 444 days. President Carter loses his re-election bid in part because of his inability to resolve the crisis. The hostages are freed on President Reagan's inauguration day.

Ayatollah Khomeini

1980s The United States and other nations decide to help the rebels (Mujahideen) in Afghanistan by supplying weapons and training to fight the Soviet troops. Osama bin Ladin is among those Mujahideen, mainly providing his money and leadership.

Iraq and Iran are at war with each other for most of the 1980s. President Saddam Hussein of Iraq uses nerve gas during the war with Iran and at the end of the war against the Kurds in northern Iraq, killing 5,000 people, and debilitating 10,000 more.

1983 A Hezbollah bomb explodes killing 241 U.S. Marines in their barracks during a

Iranians Showing Support for Hostage-taking

peacekeeping mission in Lebanon. President Reagan pulls the Marines out of Lebanon in response, making the U.S. appear weak.

1988 A bomb explodes on a U.S. bound Pan Am 747 resulting in the deaths of 271 people in Lockerbie, Scotland. Libya later acknowledges responsibility for the bombing.

1989 After nearly a decade of fighting, the Soviet Union comes to see the futility of its involvement in Afghanistan and decides to leave the country. The Soviets and the U.S. agree not to interfere in Afghanistan's politics or government. However, weapons continue to flow in to both sides of the Afghan political conflict.

1990 Iraq invades Kuwait because Kuwait would not forgive Iraq's war debt from the Iran-Iraq War.

1991 A military coalition of thirty countries with the United States as the leader is assembled by President George H.W. Bush and through a long bombing campaign and short invasion by ground troops, evicts Iraq from Kuwait. Saudi Arabia allows coalition forces to use bases in its country. This is a point of great distress to the Saudi native Osama bin Laden and his followers.

The Soviet Union is formally dissolved after nearly 70 years of oppressive rule.

1993 The first bombing of the World Trade Center. Six people are killed and 1,000 people are injured. Investigated and tried as a criminal act by the Clinton administration.

American helicopters are shot down in Somalia leading to U.S. withdrawal from that dysfunctional, war-torn African "nation". While there is good reason to question why we are there in the first place, the withdrawal of the troops by President Clinton again is a blow to perceived U.S. resolve and military prowess.

1995 A car bomb explodes in Riyadh outside a joint Saudi-U.S. facility for training Saudi national guard. Five Americans and two Indians are killed. Saudi Arabia quickly finds and executes some suspects without giving American officials a chance to interrogate and investigate the suspects' guilt.

The Alfred P. Murrah Federal building in Oklahoma City, Oklahoma is bombed by anti-government extremists Timothy Mcveigh and Terry Nicohls killing 168 people and injuring hundreds of other people.

1996 Osama Bin Laden leaves Sudan where he'd lived since being run out of Saudi Arabia. Now he is persona non grata in Sudan and he sets up shop in Afghanistan where he forges an alliance with the Taliban. With a lot of weapons and a power vacuum in the country, much of Afghanistan is taken over in 1996 by the extremist Islamic group. The Taliban is a repressive, backwards, intolerant, and ruthless sect bent on subordinating women, and destroying the people and cultures of other religions, and imposing their harsh brand of Sharia Islamic law. The Taliban give bin Laden free reign to create al Qaeda jihadist training bases in Afghanistan.

A large truck bomb explodes in the Khobar Towers residential buildings in Dhahran, Saudi Arabia killing 19 Americans and wounding 372 people.

1998 Osama bin Laden, Ayman al Zawahiri, and others publish a fatwa (Islamic religious proclamation) in a London newspaper which called for the murder of any American, anywhere on Earth, as the "individual duty for every Muslim who can do it in any country in which it is possible to do it."

Simultaneous bombings at U.S. embassies in Nairobi, Kenya and Dar es Salaam, Tanzania. The attack on the U.S. embassy in Nairobi killed 213 people, just 12 of whom were Americans, most of the rest of the dead being Kenyans. About 5,000 people were injured. The attack on the U.S. embassy in Tanzania killed 11 more people but no Americans.

U.S. demands extradition of Osama bin Laden and the Taliban refuses. Cruise missiles are fired into Afghanistan to destroy terrorist training bases run by Osama bin Ladin in response to the embassy bombings.

1999 Training begins for the operatives who would become the terrorist hijackers in al Qaeda's "Planes Operation."

2000 The USS Cole is rammed by a 35-foot boat laden with explosives and two suicide bombers on board while the battleship is refueling at a port on the coast of Yemen. Seventeen Navy crewman are killed and 47 injured.

The first operatives in al Qaeda's Planes Operation arrive in the United States.

Cruise Missile Launch

9/11

On the morning of September 11, 2001, the United States is attacked by terrorists using four fully-fueled passenger airliners as weapons of mass destruction and sacrificing the lives of hundreds of people on those planes as they were crashed at more than 500 miles per hour into the World Trade Center towers, the Pentagon, and a field in Pennsylvania. The actions of the passengers of United Flight 93, informed as they were by the other hijackings and crashes, minimized the potential for more death and destruction through their heroic actions to abort the terrorists' plot to fly the last plane into the U.S. Capitol or White House. The attacks killed nearly 3,000 people from ninety-three nations.

6:45-7:40 a.m. In Boston, Mohammed Atta, Abdul Aziz al Omari, Satam al Suqami, Wail al Shehri, and Waleed al Shehri board American Airlines Flight 11 bound for Los Angeles.

7:25 In Boston, Marwan al Shehhi, Fayez Banihammad, Mohand al Shehri, Ahmed al Ghamdi, and Hamza al Ghamdi board United Airlines Flight 175 bound for Los Angeles.

7:30-7:50 At Washington D.C.'s Dulles International Airport, Khalid al Mihdhar, Majed Moqed, Hani Hanjour, Nawaf al Hazmi, and Salem al Hazmi board American Airlines Flight 77 bound for Los Angeles.

7:40 At Newark International Airport, Saeed al Ghamdi, Ahmed al Nami, Ahmad al Haznawi, and Ziad Jarrah board United Airlines Flight 93 bound for Los Angeles.

7:59 American Airlines Flight 11 takes off from Boston's Logan Airport.

8:14 United Airlines Flight 175 takes off from Boston's Logan Airport.

8:15 American Airlines Flight 11 hijacking begins to take place.

8:20 American Airlines Flight 77 takes off from Washington Dulles International Airport.

8:42 United Airlines Flight 93 takes off from Newark International Airport.

8:43 United Airlines Flight 175 hijacking begins to take place.

8:46 American Airlines Flight 11 crashes into the North Tower of the World Trade Center.

8:51 American Airlines Flight 77 hijacking begins to take place.

9:03 United Airlines Flight 175 crashes into the South Tower of the World Trade Center.

9:25 All civilian air traffic in the United States is ordered grounded.

9:28 United Airlines Flight 93 hijacking begins to take place.

9:37 American Airlines Flight 77 crashes into the Pentagon.

9:59 The South Tower of the World Trade Center collapses.

10:03 United Airlines Flight 93 crashes into a field in Shanksville, Pennsylvania.

10:28 The North Tower of the World Trade Center collapses.

5:21 p.m. The 7 World Trade Center building collapses from damage sustained from the Twin Towers collapses.

8:30 President Bush addresses the nation from the White House concerning the attack on the U.S.

After 9/11

9/13/2001 Planes are once more allowed to fly as the national airspace is reopened to civilian air traffic.

9/17/2001 The U.S. financial markets reopen.

9/20/2001 President Bush addresses the nation before a joint session of Congress, gives the Taliban an ultimatum, and draws America's line in the sand against terrorism. "We will make no distinction between the terrorists who committed these acts and those who harbor them."

9/22/2001 Office of Homeland Security formed.

10/7/2001 The first military airstrikes occur against the Taliban in Afghanistan.

10/26/2001 The Patriot Act, an intelligence gathering and sharing law, is signed by the President.

11/13/2001 The Taliban flee Kabul, the capital of Afghanistan as opposition forces like the Northern Alliance and an increasing number of U.S. troops begin to gain control of Afghanistan's major urban areas.

5/30/2002 The last of piece of WTC steel is ceremonially removed from Ground Zero.

11/2002 Department of Homeland Security formed by an act of Congress.

2003 Khalid Sheikh Mohammed (KSM), mastermind and manager of the 9/11 plot is captured. He began his extremist career as a member of the Muslim Brotherhood in Kuwait before coming to North Carolina to earn his bachelor's degree in mechanical engineering.

In an effort to contain President Saddam Hussein and prevent his use of suspected weapons of mass destruction, the U.S. and other countries invade Iraq beginning a bloody eight-year war and occupation.

2003 Daesh (ISIL) is formed and participates in insurgent attacks against the western forces in Iraq.

2004 The publication of *The 9/11 Commission Report*.

2006 Preliminary work begins on One World Trade Center (Freedom Tower).

Former President Saddam Hussein is tried by an interim Iraqi government and hanged for his crimes against humanity.

9/11/2008 Pentagon September 11 memorial dedicated.

5/1/2011 Osama bin Laden is killed in a raid on his compound in Pakistan, where he has been living for years, by a team of U.S. special forces.

9/10/2011 The 9/11 memorials at the World Trade Center, Shanksville Pennsylvania, and at Liberty State Park, New Jersey are dedicated and open to the public.

5/5/2012 Military tribunal of Khalid Sheikh Mohammed and four other top al Qaeda terrorists begins at the military base at Guantanamo Bay, Cuba.

9/11/2012 Islamist militants attack U.S. consulate in Benghazi, Libya, killing 4 Americans and 7 Libyans including the American ambassador.

2013 Rising up from the site of the 2001 terrorist attacks, the new One World Trade Center is complete.

2014 The September 11 Museum at the World Trade Center site opens to the public.

2017 The war in Afghanistan is not won. The Taliban still attacks Afghan government forces and its U.S. advisors in its bid to regain control of Afghanistan and reinstitute its extreme brand of Islam.

Gains have been made in Iraq and Syria against Daesh but they continue to attack soft targets around the world as well as fight in Iraq and Syria. Islamic extremist terrorism seems to in no way be declining with attacks nearly every day in some part of the world.

World Trade Center Tribute in Light

One World Trade Center

The National Memorials

National 9/11 Memorial at the World Trade Center, New York City

New York, New York

> The National September 11 Memorial is a tribute of remembrance and honor to the nearly 3,000 people killed in the terror attacks of September 11, 2001 at the World Trade Center site, near Shanksville, Pennsylvania, and at the Pentagon, as well as the six people killed in the World Trade Center bombing in February 1993.
>
> The Memorial's twin reflecting pools are each nearly an acre in size and feature the largest manmade waterfalls in the North America. The pools sit within the footprints where the Twin Towers once stood. Architect Michael Arad and landscape architect Peter Walker created the memorial design selected from a global design competition that included more than 5,200 entries from 63 nations.
>
> The names of every person who died in the 2001 and 1993 attacks are inscribed into bronze panels edging the memorial pools, a powerful reminder of the largest loss of life resulting from a foreign attack on American soil and the greatest single loss of rescue personnel in American history. (*from* www.911memorial.org) **Dedicated**: September 10, 2011

The construction of the September 11 museum, pictured here behind the north reflecting pool (shown in 2011), was opened to the public in 2014. The museum structure looks like a WTC building lying down on its side. It commemorates the lives of every victim of the 1993 and 2001 attacks by telling their stories through photos, video, sound, artifacts, and words. The memorial's grounds (pictured below) are expansive, park-like and almost serene in the midst of busy downtown Manhattan. Security procedures to get into the museum rival that of a TSA shakedown at the airport. The incomplete One World Trade Center tower (a.k.a., Freedom Tower) can be seen behind the 9/11 Memorial Museum. The Freedom Tower was completed in 2013, becoming the tallest building in the Western Hemisphere at 1776 feet.

This photograph of the fall of water in one of the reflecting pools doesn't come close to conveying the immensity of these waterfalls and the thunderous sound as the water hits the pool bottom. In fact, 40,000 gallons of water per minute fall a total distance of 46 feet (30 feet and then 16 feet). Some of this water rises back up into the air around the two pools as mist in the same way that many natural waterfalls produce mist in the air around them.

The sun, the mist, and the wind all combine to create photographic challenges or benefits, depending on how you look at it.

If you want to take effective pictures at any of the national memorials, it's important to have a digital camera with a decent optical zoom lens (8x or more). An SLR (digital or film) with a good telephoto lens is even better. The authors used both.

A nonturbulent shelf of water spills over a ledge to create the memorial's sheer waterfalls, the largest manmade waterfalls in North America.

On a sunny day there is a surplus of light reflection off of all the glass-covered buildings in the area. Don't forget to bring your sunglasses and camera filters.

There are visitors of many nationalities among the millions of people who have visited the National September 11 World Trade Center Memorial and Museum. Visitors have also come from every state in the U.S.

The authors had seen pictures of the memorial prior to their visit, but were in no way prepared for the size and scale of its presentation. It is a humbling space. Notice how small the people are on the other side of the reflecting pool.

The names of all those people who died in the tragedy of September 11, 2001 are etched into a bronze counter that wraps around the top of each reflecting pool. Touch is a strong component of visiting this memorial as it is at most 9/11 memorials. The names here are etched deeply into the bronze providing a strong tactile connection to the names of the victims. Roses are placed into the names of victims on their birthdays.

On sunny days, the reflections of the surrounding buildings can be seen in the top shelf of water of the reflecting pools as well as in the mirrored glass of the surrounding buildings.

The Museum, with 110,000 square feet of exhibition space, was mired in controversy over what to display and what not to display and funding disputes which according to *The New York Times* "will delay the opening of the Museum until 2013". Delay has been par for the course as regards nearly every aspect of development at the World Trade Center site. The museum was finally opened to the public in May of 2014.

When you come out of the World Trade Center PATH and subway station you are greeted with this view of the 9/11 Museum. The memorial and memorial property can be accessed by just walking on to the open property. To go inside the museum, you need to purchase a ticket which can be done online before you get there, at an ATM-like kiosk on site, or at a ticket window, where the line on this Thursday in August was fairly long. Once inside there is a TSA-like security check and then you can proceed inside to explore the space on your own, or with a tour if you pay for that option.

The first thing you see as you enter the museum space are these twin fork support beams from the wreckage of the World Trade Center. Most of the museum is underground and gets deeper as you proceed through it.

The Last Column was an impromptu symbol and memorial for the first responders who were part of the rescue and recovery efforts at Ground Zero. Behind that is the concrete retaining wall that kept the waters of the Hudson River from encroaching on the foundation and basements of the World Trade Center.

There are many artifacts in the museum including part of the broken radio antenna from the top of the North Tower, a fire truck which was crushed when the buildings collapsed, an elevator motor from one of the buildings and foundation supports. There are also rooms which remember the victims with a photo of each person on the walls and searches for information about each of the victims may be done on memorial kiosk screens in these rooms. A quotation dedicated to the victims and surrounded by blue tiles representing the blue sky of September 11, 2001 graces a wall deep within the museum space. It reads: No day shall erase you from the memory of time.

Aerial view of the WTC memorial site, September 2017.

Names etched into bronze counter around the reflecting pools.

The Pentagon 9/11 Memorial

The Pentagon 9/11 Memorial

> The National 9/11 Pentagon Memorial in Arlington County, Virginia preserves the memories of 184 lives extinguished by terrorists who slammed a fully fueled Boeing 757 into the Pentagon. The memorial consists of simple aerodynamic benches, each representing a victim of the attack, that give the feeling of flight and are lined up with the trajectory of American Airlines Flight 77 as it headed towards the building at 530 miles per hour. The benches that represent the 125 Pentagon deaths face one way and the benches that represent the 59 Flight 77 deaths face the other. They are also lined up by age from one side of the memorial park to the other.
>
> Each bench has its own reflecting pool of water and victims from the same family are linked together by a plaque at the end of the pool of water, which lists their family members who also died in the attack. The Pentagon Memorial was the first of the national memorials to be dedicated. Construction began in June of 2006 with the dedication ceremony taking place on September 11, 2008.

Inscriptions: We claim this ground in remembrance of the events of September 11, 2001. To honor the 184 people whose lives were lost, their families, and all who sacrifice that we may live in freedom. We will never forget.

We will be forever grateful to the thousands of people from across the nation and around the world who contributed their time, resources and energy to create this Memorial.

On September 11, 2001, acts of terrorism took the lives of the thousands at the World Trade Center in New York City, in a grassy field in Shanksville, Pennsylvania and here at the Pentagon. We will forever remember our loved ones, friends and colleagues.

The Entry Stone to Pentagon Memorial, above; The Locator Stone lists those who died and the year they were born, below.

An example of the connections between memorials. Victims from the same family are linked to each other by this plaque at the end of the pool water in each individual memorial.

Individual memorials consist of aerodynamically-styled stainless-steel benches inlaid with smooth granite.

There is also a lighted pool of flowing water (next page) underneath each memorial bench and a permanent tribute, by name, to each victim on the end of the bench.

The water flows continuously under each monument. Every morning, however, at 9:37, the flowing water is turned off in a moment of silence for the 184 lives lost at the Pentagon.

The memorials sit in a large field of gravel sharing space with eighty-five small Crape Myrtle trees. As the trees grow this place is going to have a very different feel to it than the open airiness that it has now.

Some areas of the memorial park are more sparsely populated by individual monuments than others due to there being few victims in those age ranges.

The individual memorials' alignment with the Pentagon can be seen here.

The low stone wall (or bench) on the right in this photograph has year markers for each of the age lines that run towards the Pentagon along the flight path of Flight 77.

Behind this stone wall is a rising concrete Age Wall which starts at 3 inches and rises to 71 inches to symbolize the age range of the victims of the tragedy.

The brick path here and the alignment of all the memorials indicate the path American Airlines Flight 77 took towards its impact with the Pentagon.

Memorial wreaths adorn some individual benches, as left by family members or friends.

The memorial units to the left of this path are for the thirteen oldest victims at the Pentagon Memorial, the youngest being 65 and the oldest being 71 years of age.

A floral wreath laid on a victim's memorial bench by family or friend.

The daytime reflection off the water below may be seen on the memorial benches in this photograph.

The lighted pool of water beneath each stainless-steel memorial bench makes for a surreal nighttime atmosphere at the Pentagon memorial park.

A seascape of memorial benches appears like so many swimming shark fins.

Looking out to the western sky where the hijacked American Airlines Flight 77 came in towards the Pentagon at more than 500 miles per hour. The United States Air Force Memorial can be seen in the distance outside the Pentagon complex and across I-395. Coincidentally, the USAF memorial is roughly in the flight path that American Airlines Flight 77 took to impact the building. The USAF memorial was dedicated in October 2006 and is itself an impressive memorial worth visiting in the Washington, D.C. area.

The Pentagon Memorial is organized as a timeline of the victims' ages, spanning from 3-year-old Dana Falkenberg to 71-year-old John D. Yamnicky. Each individual memorial bench is located on its respective age line. The benches are then organized by birth date along the line. The age lines traverse the park at about a 45-degree angle to the Pentagon, tracing the path of American Airlines Flight 77 as it flew into the building. The low stone wall here demarcates each line with a year.

The eighty-five Crape Myrtle trees will grow to over thirty-feet tall providing a shady park for reflection and homes to many birds. As shade trees, these are just babies compared to the giants they'll become.

The Pentagon Memorial design was developed by Julie Beckman and Keith Kaseman.

Flight 93 National Memorial, Shanksville, Pennsylvania

Flight 93 National Memorial, Shanksville, Pennsylvania

> Phase 1 of the Flight 93 National Memorial is complete. It is anticipated that phase 2 will be done by 2018. However, there is enough to see and revere if you go now – as much, or more in fact than many "complete" memorials. There is the Memorial Plaza and its marble wall with the forty names of the passengers and crew of United Flight 93 inscribed upon it. The Memorial wall follows the path of Flight 93 as it headed towards its crash. There is also a visitor's center where you can sign a visitor's book and look at a timeline of events and read personal statements. National Park Service rangers are on hand to assist and answer questions. It is worth the trip into the beautiful hinterlands of Pennsylvania.

A view from the platform towards the Flight 93 crash site. The inscription in the glass on the platform reads: A common field one day, a field of honor forever.

Dedicated: September 10, 2011

Special Info: Our visit was also very windy and bitterly cold for September, perhaps due to the altitude of this place (a dozen or so wind turbines can be seen on the distant hills). So go dressed for the weather if it's between September and May. While you're in Somerset County, Pennsylvania, go and visit the architect Frank Lloyd Wright's Falling Water House. It's not far and is well worth the trip. But call ahead as the tours sell out ahead of time.

The Visitor Shelter at the Memorial Plaza, above; Parking lot, below.

The low wall on the left of the above picture prevents visitors from accessing the restricted final resting place of the heroes of Flight 93. When it's cold and windy, it's a long walk from the Visitor Shelter to the Memorial Wall of Names.

This photo was taken from the Visitor Center. It looks toward the Memorial Plaza. The white Wall of Names is on the right side of the picture and points toward the boulder that marks the spot of the crash site near the tree line.

Now known as the Field of Heroes, the site of the crash of United Airlines Flight 93 is part of land that was a former surface coal mine. A low wall prevents visitors from accessing the actual crash site near the rock shown below. Family members of victims of the crash can access the crash site directly.

The large rock at the site is adorned with stones, pebbles, flags, flowers and other memorial tokens left by family members.

A crater fifteen feet deep by thirty feet wide was created by the plane's impact. This crater was filled with soil and seeded with grass and wildflowers after the investigation of the site was complete.

The Wall of Names

The Wall of Names consists of forty white marble panels inscribed with the names of the passengers and crew of Flight 93. The black granite walkway along the wall marks the direction of the flight path.

The best views of the crash site can be had with binoculars or a good telephoto camera lens through the ceremonial gate shown here. In our opinion, with all the granite and marble around this memorial, the simple wooden gate seems kind of out of place.

Unfortunately, this memorial is the only one of the scores of 9/11 memorials we have been to where binoculars or a good telephoto lens are helpful to see a portion of the memorial. The Wall of Names traces a portion of the plane's path until it reaches the ceremonial gate.

About 265,000 visitors came to pay their respects at the Flight 93 National Memorial in 2011.

Flowers line the base of the Wall of Names on a blustery fall day. As with nearly every 9/11 memorial, people continue to bring flowers or personal mementos.

Boston's Logan International Airport, Boston, Massachusetts

Boston's Logan International Airport, Boston Massachusetts

The Place of Remembrance, the September 11 memorial at Boston's Logan International Airport is one of the most beautiful and most unusual 9/11 memorials in the U.S. The memorial site consists of an inscripted plaza with seating, a reflective pathway, and a large glass sculpture that features two glass panels etched with the names of the passengers and crew of each flight which took off from that airport to crash into the World Trade Center. This memorial is not easy to find or see unless you are specifically on a hunt to see it, or if you are staying at the Hilton Hotel across the parking lot from it. Even if you are taking a flight somewhere from this airport, it is not something that you'd just come across very easily. It is worth finding if you are in Boston though.

Dedicated: September 9, 2008

Special Info: American Airlines Flight 11 and United Airlines Flight 175, the airplanes used by the terrorists as weapons of mass destruction to bring down the World Trade Center, took off bound for Los Angeles from Boston at 7:59 a.m. and 8:14 a.m.

The view from an upper level of the airport's parking garage. Visitors can follow one of two winding walkways in the 2.5-acre park that echo the flight paths of Flight 11 and Flight 175, as they make their way through a grove of Ginkgo trees to The Place of Remembrance.

The plaza is the entrance to the memorial. After reflecting on the inscription in the granite here, visitors can follow one of the two paths to the main part of the memorial. One of the intentions of this memorial is that the visitor to it "Remember this Day". However, nowhere at the memorial does it mention what the events were. Therefore, the memorial relies on the mass consciousness of the event rather than supplying the information as to what is to be remembered. The people who died are recognized on glass panels, but again, no reason is offered.

Inscription in Plaza: Remember this Day. This memorial is intended as a place of reflection for all those who were forever changed by the events of September 11, 2001

The green-hued glass memorial as it appears during the day and at night. Access is available 24/7.

The roof of the memorial is made up of shards of glass suspended in air by light steel cables. The shards are meant to represent a fractured sky.

United Airlines Flight 175

Crew

Victor Saracini, Captain
Michael Horrocks, First Officer

Flight Attendants

Robert J. Fangman
Amy Nicole Jarret
Amy R. King
Kathryn L. LaBorie

Alfred G. Marchand
Michael C. Tarrou
Alicia Titus

Passengers

Alona Avraham
Garnet "Ace" Bailey
Mark Lawrence Bavis
Graham Berkeley
Touri Bolourchi
Klaus Bothe
Daniel Brandhorst
David Brandhorst
John B. Cahill
Christoffer M. Carstanjen
John "Jay" Corcoran
Dorothy de Araujo
Gloria DeBarrera
Lisa Frost
Ronald Gamboa
Lynn Catherine Goodchild
Peter M. Goodrich
Douglas A. Gowell
Rev. Francis Grogan
Christine Lee Hanson
Peter Burton Hanson
Sue Kim Hanson
Gerald Hardacre
Eric Hartono
James E. Hayden
Herbert Wilson Homer

Robert A. Jalbert
Ralph F. Kershaw
Heinrich Kimmig
Brian Kevin Kinney
Robert G. LeBlanc
Maclovio Lopez
Marianne MacFarlane ✈
L. "Neil" Mariani
Brandeis McBratney
Juliana Valentine McCourt
Ruth Clifford McCourt
Wolfgang Menzel
Shawn M. Nassaney
Marie Pappalardo
Patrick J. Quigley IV
Fred Rimmele MD
James M. Roux
Jesus "JR" Sanchez ✈
Kathleen Shearer
Robert M. Shearer
Jane Louise Simpkin
Brian David Sweeney
Deborah Tavolarella
Timothy Ward
William Michael Weems

✈ *United Airlines Employee*

American Airlines Flight 11

Crew

John Ogonowski, Captain
Thomas F. McGuinness Jr., First Officer

Flight Attendants

Barbara Arestegui
Jeffrey D. Collman
Sara Low
Karen Martin
Kathleen Ann Nicosia

Betty Ann Ong
Jean D. Roger
Dianne Bullis Snyder
Madeline Amy Sweeney

Passengers

Anna S.W. Allison
David Angell
Lynn Angell
Seima Aoyama
Myra Aronson
Christine Johnna Barbuto
Carol Beug
Kelly Booms
Carol Bouchard
Neilie Anne Heffernan Casey
Jeffrey William Coombs
Tara Kathleen Creamer
Thelma Cuccinello
Patrick J. Currivan
Brian Dale
David DiMeglio
Donald A. DiTullio
Alberto Domínguez
Alexander M. Filipov
Carol Flyzik
Paul J. Friedman
Karleton Douglas Beye Fyfe
Peter A. Gay
Linda Mae George
Edmund Glazer
Lisa Fenn Gordenstein
Andrew Curry Green
Paige Farley Hackel
Peter P. Hashem
Robert J. Hayes
Edward R. Hennessy, Jr.
John Hofer
Cora Hidalgo Holland
John Nicholas Humber
Waleed Joseph Iskandar
John Jenkins
Col. Charles E. Jones
Robin L. Kaplan

Barbara A. Keating
David P. Kovalcin
Judy C. Larocque
Natalie "Janis" Lasden
Daniel John Lee
Daniel Lewin
Susan McAleney Mackay
Christopher Daniel Mello
Jeffrey Mladenik
Antonio Montoya
Carlos Montoya
Laura Lee Defazio Morabito
Mildred Rose Naiman
Laurie Olsen Neira
Renee Tetreault Newell
Jacqueline Norton
Robert Norton
Jane M. Orth
Thomas Nicholas Pecorelli
Berinthia Berenson Perkins
Sonia Mercedes Morales Puopolo
David E. Retik
Philip M. Rosenzweig
Richard Barry Ross
Jessica Leigh Sachs
Rahma Salie
Heather Smith
Douglas Stone
Xavier Suarez
Michael Theodoridis
Jim Trentini
Mary Trentini
Pendy Vamsikrish
Mary Wahlstrom
Kenneth E. Waldie
John J. Wenckus
Candace Lee Williams
Christopher R. Zarba, Jr.

The Victims of September 11, 2001

World Trade Center Victims

Gordon M. Aamoth, Jr.
Edelmiro Abad
Maria Rose Abad
Andrew Anthony Abate
Vincent Abate
Laurence Christopher Abel
William F. Abrahamson
Richard Anthony Aceto
Jesus Acevedo Rescand
Heinrich Bernhard Ackermann
Paul Acquaviva
Donald LaRoy Adams
Patrick Adams
Shannon Lewis Adams
Stephen George Adams
Ignatius Udo Adanga
Christy A. Addamo
Terence E. Adderley, Jr.
Sophia Buruwad Addo
Lee Allan Adler
Daniel Thomas Afflitto
Emmanuel Akwasi Afuakwah
Alok Agarwal
Mukul Kumar Agarwala
Joseph Agnello
David Scott Agnes
Brian G. Ahearn
Jeremiah Joseph Ahern
Joanne Marie Ahladiotis
Shabbir Ahmed
Terrance Andre Aiken
Godwin Ajala
Gertrude M. Alagero
Andrew Alameno
Margaret Ann Alario
Gary M. Albero
Jon Leslie Albert
Peter Alderman
Jacquelyn Delaine Aldridge
David D. Alger
Sarah Ali-Escarcega
Ernest Alikakos
Edward L. Allegretto
Eric Allen
Joseph Ryan Allen
Richard Dennis Allen
Richard Lanard Allen
Christopher E. Allingham
Janet M. Alonso
Arturo Alva-Moreno
Anthony Alvarado

Antonio Javier Alvarez
Victoria Alvarez-Brito
Telmo E. Alvear
Cesar Amoranto Alviar
Tariq Amanullah
Angelo Amaranto
James M. Amato Joseph Amatuccio
Christopher Charles Amoroso
Kazuhiro Anai
Calixto Anaya, Jr.
Joseph Anchundia
Kermit Charles Anderson
Yvette Constance Anderson
John Andreacchio
Michael Rourke Andrews
Jean Ann Andrucki
Siew-Nya Ang
Joseph Angelini, Jr.
Joseph Angelini, Sr.
Laura Angilletta
Doreen J. Angrisani
Lorraine Antigua
Peter Paul Apollo
Faustino Apostol, Jr.
Frank Thomas Aquilino
Patrick Michael Aranyos
David Arce
Michael George Arczynski
Louis Arena
Adam P. Arias
Michael Armstrong
Jack Charles Aron
Joshua Aron
Richard Avery Aronow
Japhet Jesse Aryee
Patrick Asante
Carl Asaro
Michael Asciak
Michael Edward Asher
Janice Marie Ashley
Thomas J. Ashton
Manuel O. Asitimbay
Gregg Arthur Atlas
Gerald T. Atwood
James Audiffred
Louis Frank Aversano, Jr.
Ezra Aviles
Sandy Ayala
Arlene T. Babakitis
Eustace P. Bacchus
John J. Badagliacca
Jane Ellen Baeszler
Robert J. Baierwalter

Andrew J. Bailey
Brett T. Bailey
Tatyana Bakalinskaya
Michael S. Baksh
Sharon M. Balkcom
Michael Andrew Bane
Katherine Bantis
Gerard Baptiste
Walter Baran
Gerard A. Barbara
Paul Vincent Barbaro
James William Barbella
Ivan Kyrillos F. Barbosa
Victor Daniel Barbosa
Colleen Ann Barkow
David Michael Barkway
Matthew Barnes
Sheila Patricia Barnes
Evan J. Baron
Renee Barrett-Arjune
Nathaly Barrios La Cruz
Arthur Thaddeus Barry
Diane G. Barry
Maurice Vincent Barry
Scott D. Bart
Carlton W. Bartels
Guy Barzvi
Inna B. Basina
Alysia Basmajian
Kenneth William Basnicki
Steven Bates
Paul James Battaglia
Walter David Bauer, Jr.
Marlyn Capito Bautista
Jasper Baxter
Michele Beale
Paul Frederick Beatini
Jane S. Beatty
Lawrence Ira Beck
Manette Marie Beckles
Carl John Bedigian
Michael Earnest Beekman
Maria A. Behr
Yelena Belilovsky
Nina Patrice Bell
Debbie Bellows
Stephen Elliot Belson
Paul M. Benedetti
Denise Lenore Benedetto
Maria Bengochea
Bryan Craig Bennett
Eric L. Bennett
Oliver Duncan Bennett

Margaret L. Benson
Dominick J. Berardi
James Patrick Berger
Steven Howard Berger
John P. Bergin
Alvin Bergsohn
Daniel Bergstein
Michael J. Berkeley
Donna M. Bernaerts
David W. Bernard
William Bernstein
David M. Berray
David S. Berry
Joseph J. Berry
William Reed Bethke
Timothy Betterly
Edward Frank Beyea
Paul Beyer
Anil Tahilram Bharvaney
Bella J. Bhukhan
Shimmy D. Biegeleisen
Peter Alexander Bielfeld
William G. Biggart
Brian Bilcher
Carl Vincent Bini
Gary Eugene Bird
Joshua David Birnbaum
George John Bishop
Jeffrey Donald Bittner
Albert Balewa Blackman, Jr.
Christopher Joseph Blackwell
Susan Leigh Blair
Harry Blanding, Jr.
Janice Lee Blaney
Craig Michael Blass
Rita Blau
Richard Middleton Blood, Jr.
Michael Andrew Boccardi
John P. Bocchi
Michael Leopoldo Bocchino
Susan M. Bochino
Bruce D. Boehm
Mary Catherine Boffa
Nicholas Andrew Bogdan
Darren Christopher Bohan
Lawrence Francis Boisseau
Vincent M. Boland, Jr.
Alan Bondarenko
Andre Bonheur, Jr.
Colin Arthur Bonnett
Frank Bonomo
Yvonne Lucia Bonomo
Genieve Bonsignore, 3
Seaon Booker
Sherry Ann Bordeaux
Krystine Bordenabe
Martin Boryczewski
Richard Edward Bosco
John H. Boulton
Francisco Eligio Bourdier
Thomas Harold Bowden, Jr.

Kimberly S. Bowers
Veronique Nicole Bowers
Larry Bowman
Shawn Edward Bowman, Jr.
Kevin L. Bowser
Gary R. Box
Gennady Boyarsky
Pamela Boyce
Michael Boyle
Alfred Braca
Kevin Bracken
David Brian Brady
Alexander Braginsky
Nicholas W. Brandemarti
Michelle Renee Bratton
Patrice Braut
Lydia E. Bravo
Ronald Michael Breitweiser
Edward A. Brennan III
Francis Henry Brennan
Michael E. Brennan
Peter Brennan
Thomas M. Brennan
Daniel J. Brethel
Gary Lee Bright
Jonathan Briley
Mark A. Brisman
Paul Gary Bristow
Mark Francis Broderick
Herman Charles Broghammer
Keith A. Broomfield
Ethel Brown Janice
Juloise Brown
Lloyd Stanford Brown
Patrick J. Brown
Bettina Browne
Mark Bruce
Richard George Bruehert
Andrew Brunn
Vincent Brunton
Ronald Paul Bucca
Brandon J. Buchanan
Gregory Joseph Buck
Dennis Buckley
Nancy Clare Bueche
Patrick Joseph Buhse
John Edwards Bulaga, Jr.
Stephen Bunin
Matthew J. Burke
Thomas Daniel Burke
William Francis Burke, Jr.
Donald J. Burns
Kathleen Anne Burns
Keith James Burns
John Patrick Burnside
Irina Buslo
Milton G. Bustillo
Thomas M. Butler
Patrick Byrne
Timothy G. Byrne
Jesus Neptali Cabezas

Lillian Caceres
Brian Joseph Cachia
Steven Dennis Cafiero, Jr.
Richard M. Caggiano
Cecile Marella Caguicla
Michael John Cahill
Scott Walter Cahill
Thomas Joseph Cahill
George Cain
Salvatore B. Calabro
Joseph Calandrillo
Philip V. Calcagno
Edward Calderon
Kenneth Marcus Caldwell
Dominick Enrico Calia
Felix Calixte
Frank Callahan
Liam Callahan
Luigi Calvi
Roko Camaj
Michael F. Cammarata
David Otey Campbell
Geoffrey Thomas Campbell
Jill Marie Campbell
Robert Arthur Campbell
Sandra Patricia Campbell
Sean Thomas Canavan
John A. Candela
Vincent Cangelosi
Stephen J. Cangialosi
Lisa Bella Cannava
Brian Cannizzaro
Michael Canty
Louis Anthony Caporicci
Jonathan Neff Cappello
James Christopher Cappers
Richard Michael Caproni
Jose Manuel Cardona
Dennis M. Carey
Steve Carey
Edward Carlino
Michael Scott Carlo
David G. Carlone
Rosemarie C. Carlson
Mark Stephen Carney
Joyce Ann Carpeneto
Ivhan Luis Carpio Bautista
Jeremy M. Carrington
Michael Carroll
Peter Carroll
James Joseph Carson, Jr.
Marcia Cecil Carter
James Marcel Cartier
Vivian Casalduc
John Francis Casazza
Paul R. Cascio
Margarito Casillas
Thomas Anthony Casoria
William Otto Caspar
Alejandro Castano
Arcelia Castillo

Germaan Castillo Garcia
Leonard M. Castrianno
Jose Ramon Castro
Richard G. Catarelli
Christopher Sean Caton
Robert John Caufield
Mary Teresa Caulfield
Judson Cavalier
Michael Joseph Cawley
Jason David Cayne
Juan Armando Ceballos
Jason Michael Cefalu
Thomas Joseph Celic
Ana Mercedes Centeno
Joni Cesta
Jeffrey Marc Chairnoff
Swarna Chalasani
William Chalcoff
Eli Chalouh
Charles Lawrence Chan
Mandy Chang
Mark Lawrence Charette
Gregorio Manuel Chavez
Delrose E. Cheatham
Pedro Francisco Checo
Douglas MacMillan Cherry
Stephen Patrick Cherry
Vernon Paul Cherry
Nester Julio Chevalier
Swede Chevalier
Alexander H. Chiang
Dorothy J. Chiarchiaro
Luis Alfonso Chimbo
Robert Chin
Wing Wai Ching
Nicholas Paul Chiofalo
John Chipura
Peter A. Chirchirillo
Catherine Chirls
Kyung Hee Cho
Abul K. Chowdhury
Mohammad Salahuddin Chowdhury
Kirsten L. Christophe
Pamela Chu
Steven Chucknick
Wai Chung
Christopher Ciafardini
Alex F. Ciccone
Frances Ann Cilente
Elaine Cillo
Edna Cintron
Nestor Andre Cintron III
Robert Dominick Cirri
Juan Pablo Cisneros-Alvarez
Benjamin Keefe Clark
Eugene Clark
Gregory Alan Clark
Mannie Leroy Clark
Thomas R. Clark
Christopher Robert Clarke
Donna Marie Clarke

Michael J. Clarke
Suria Rachel Emma Clarke
Kevin Francis Cleary
James D. Cleere
Geoffrey W. Cloud
Susan Marie Clyne
Steven Coakley
Jeffrey Alan Coale
Patricia A. Cody
Daniel Michael Coffey
Jason M. Coffey
Florence G. Cohen
Kevin Sanford Cohen
Anthony Joseph Coladonato
Mark Joseph Colaio
Stephen Colaio
Christopher M. Colasanti
Kevin Nathaniel Colbert
Michel P. Colbert
Keith E. Coleman
Scott Thomas Coleman
Tarel Coleman
Liam Joseph Colhoun
Robert D. Colin
Robert J. Coll
Jean Collin
John Michael Collins
Michael L. Collins
Thomas J. Collins
Joseph Collison
Patricia Malia Colodner
Linda M. Colon
Sol E. Colon
Ronald Edward Comer
Sandra Jolane Conaty Brace
Jaime Concepcion
Albert Conde
Denease Conley
Susan P. Conlon
Margaret Mary Conner
Cynthia Marie Lise Connolly
John E. Connolly, Jr.
James Lee Connor
Jonathan M. Connors
Kevin Patrick Connors
Kevin F. Conroy
Jose Manuel Contreras-Fernandez
Brenda E. Conway
Dennis Michael Cook
Helen D. Cook
John A. Cooper
Joseph John Coppo, Jr.
Gerard J. Coppola
Joseph Albert Corbett
Alejandro Cordero
Robert Cordice
Ruben D. Correa
Danny A. Correa-Gutierrez
James J. Corrigan
Carlos Cortes
Kevin Cosgrove

Dolores Marie Costa
Digna Alexandra Costanza
Charles Gregory Costello, Jr.
Michael S. Costello
Conrod K. Cottoy
Martin John Coughlan
John Gerard Coughlin
Timothy J. Coughlin
James E. Cove
Andre Cox
Frederick John Cox
James Raymond Coyle
Michele Coyle-Eulau
Anne Marie Cramer
Christopher S. Cramer
Denise Elizabeth Crant
James Leslie Crawford, Jr.
Robert James Crawford
Joanne Mary Cregan
Lucy Crifasi
John A. Crisci
Daniel Hal Crisman
Dennis Cross
Kevin Raymond Crotty
Thomas G. Crotty
John Crowe
Welles Remy Crowther
Robert L. Cruikshank
John Robert Cruz
Grace Yu Cua
Kenneth John Cubas
Francisco Cruz Cubero
Richard J. Cudina
Neil James Cudmore
Thomas Patrick Cullen III
Joyce Cummings
Brian Thomas Cummins
Michael Cunningham
Robert Curatolo
Laurence Damian Curia
Paul Dario Curioli
Beverly Curry
Michael S. Curtin
Gavin Cushny
John D'Allara
Vincent Gerard D'Amadeo
Jack D'Ambrosi
Mary D'Antonio
Edward A. D'Atri
Michael D. D'Auria
Michael Jude D'Esposito
Manuel John Da Mota
Caleb Arron Dack
Carlos S. DaCosta
Joao Alberto DaFonseca Aguiar, Jr.
Thomas A. Damaskinos
Jeannine Marie Damiani-Jones
Patrick W. Danahy
Nana Danso
Vincent Danz
Dwight Donald Darcy

Elizabeth Ann Darling
Annette Andrea Dataram
Lawrence Davidson
Michael Allen Davidson
Scott Matthew Davidson
Titus Davidson
Niurka Davila
Clinton Davis
Wayne Terrial Davis
Anthony Richard Dawson
Calvin Dawson
Edward James Day
Jayceryll de Chavez
Jennifer De Jesus
Monique E. De Jesus
Nereida De Jesus
Emerita De La Pena
Azucena Maria de la Torre
David Paul De Rubbio
Jemal Legesse De Santis
Christian Louis De Simone
Melanie Louise De Vere
William Thomas Dean
Robert J. DeAngelis, Jr.
Thomas Patrick DeAngelis
Tara E. Debek
Anna Marjia DeBin
James V. Deblase
Paul DeCola
Simon Marash Dedvukaj
Jason Defazio
David A. DeFeo
Manuel Del Valle, Jr.
Donald Arthur Delapenha
Vito Joseph DeLeo
Danielle Anne Delie
Joseph A. Della Pietra
Andrea DellaBella
Palmina DelliGatti
Colleen Ann Deloughery
Francis Albert DeMartini
Anthony Demas
Martin N. DeMeo
Francis Deming
Carol K. Demitz
Kevin Dennis
Thomas F. Dennis
Jean DePalma
Jose Depena
Robert John Deraney
Michael DeRienzo
Edward DeSimone III
Andrew Desperito
Cindy Ann Deuel
Jerry DeVito
Robert P. Devitt, Jr.
Dennis Lawrence Devlin
Gerard Dewan
Sulemanali Kassamali Dhanani
Patricia Florence Di Chiaro
Debra Ann Di Martino

Michael Louis Diagostino
Matthew Diaz
Nancy Diaz
Rafael Arturo Diaz
Michael A. Diaz-Piedra III
Judith Berquis Diaz-Sierra
Joseph Dermot Dickey, Jr.
Lawrence Patrick Dickinson
Michael D. Diehl
John Difato
Vincent Difazio
Carl Anthony DiFranco
Donald Difranco
Stephen Patrick Dimino
William John Dimmling
Marisa DiNardo Schorpp
Christopher M. Dincuff
Jeffrey Mark Dingle
Anthony Dionisio
George DiPasquale
Joseph Dipilato
Douglas Frank DiStefano
Ramzi A. Doany
John Joseph Doherty
Melissa C. Doi
Brendan Dolan
Neil Matthew Dollard
James Joseph Domanico
Benilda Pascua Domingo
Carlos Dominguez
Jerome Mark Patrick Dominguez
Kevin W. Donnelly
Jacqueline Donovan
Stephen Scott Dorf
Thomas Dowd
Kevin Dowdell
Mary Yolanda Dowling
Raymond Mathew Downey
Frank Joseph Doyle
Joseph Michael Doyle
Stephen Patrick Driscoll
Mirna A. Duarte
Michelle Beale Duberry
Luke A. Dudek
Christopher Michael Duffy
Gerard Duffy
Michael Joseph Duffy
Thomas W. Duffy
Antoinette Duger
Sareve Dukat
Christopher Joseph Dunne
Richard Anthony Dunstan
Patrick Thomas Dwyer
Joseph Anthony Eacobacci
John Bruce Eagleson
Robert Douglas Eaton
Dean Phillip Eberling
Margaret Ruth Echtermann
Paul Robert Eckna
Constantine Economos
Dennis Michael Edwards

Michael Hardy Edwards
Christine Egan
Lisa Egan
Martin J. Egan, Jr.
Michael Egan
Samantha Martin Egan
Carole Eggert
Lisa Caren Ehrlich
John Ernst Eichler
Eric Adam Eisenberg
Daphne Ferlinda Elder
Michael J. Elferis
Mark Joseph Ellis
Valerie Silver Ellis
Albert Alfy William Elmarry
Edgar Hendricks Emery, Jr.
Doris Suk-Yuen Eng
Christopher Epps
Ulf Ramm Ericson
Erwin L. Erker
William John Erwin
Jose Espinal
Fanny Espinoza
Bridget Ann Esposito
Francis Esposito
Michael Esposito
William Esposito
Ruben Esquilin, Jr.
Sadie Ette
Barbara G. Etzold
Eric Brian Evans
Robert Evans
Meredith Emily June Ewart
Catherine K. Fagan
Patricia Mary Fagan
Keith George Fairben
Sandra Fajardo-Smith
William F. Fallon
William Lawrence Fallon, Jr.
Anthony J. Fallone, Jr.
Dolores Brigitte Fanelli
John Joseph Fanning
Kathleen Anne Faragher
Thomas Farino
Nancy Carole Farley
Elizabeth Ann Farmer
Douglas Jon Farnum
John G. Farrell
John W. Farrell
Terrence Patrick Farrell
Joseph D. Farrelly
Thomas Patrick Farrelly
Syed Abdul Fatha
Christopher Edward Faughnan
Wendy R. Faulkner
Shannon Marie Fava
Bernard D. Favuzza
Robert Fazio, Jr.
Ronald Carl Fazio
William Feehan
Francis Jude Feely

Garth Erin Feeney
Sean B. Fegan
Lee S. Fehling
Peter Adam Feidelberg
Alan D. Feinberg
Rosa Maria Feliciano
Edward Thomas Fergus, Jr.
George Ferguson
Henry Fernandez
Judy Hazel Fernandez
Julio Fernandez
Elisa Giselle Ferraina
Anne Marie Sallerin Ferreira
Robert John Ferris
David Francis Ferrugio
Louis V. Fersini
Michael David Ferugio
Bradley James Fetchet
Jennifer Louise Fialko
Kristen Nicole Fiedel
Samuel Fields
Michael Bradley Finnegan
Timothy J. Finnerty
Michael Curtis Fiore
Stephen S R Fiorelli, Sr.
Paul M. Fiori
John B. Fiorito
John R. Fischer
Andrew Fisher
Bennett Lawson Fisher
John Roger Fisher
Thomas J. Fisher
Lucy A. Fishman
Ryan D. Fitzgerald
Thomas James Fitzpatrick
Richard P. Fitzsimons
Salvatore Fiumefreddo
Christina Donovan Flannery
Eileen Flecha
Andre G. Fletcher
Carl M. Flickinger
John Joseph Florio
Joseph Walken Flounders
David Fodor
Michael N. Fodor
Stephen Mark Fogel
Thomas Foley
David J. Fontana
Chih Min Foo
Godwin Forde
Donald A. Foreman
Christopher Hugh Forsythe
Claudia Alicia Foster
Noel John Foster
Ana Fosteris
Robert Joseph Foti
Jeffrey Fox
Virginia Fox
Pauline Francis
Virgin Francis
Gary Jay Frank

Morton H. Frank
Peter Christopher Frank
Richard K. Fraser
Kevin J. Frawley
Clyde Frazier, Jr.
Lillian Inez Frederick
Andrew Fredricks
Tamitha Freeman
Brett Owen Freiman
Peter L. Freund
Arlene Eva Fried
Alan Wayne Friedlander
Andrew Keith Friedman
Gregg J. Froehner
Peter Christian Fry
Clement A. Fumando
Steven Elliot Furman
Paul Furmato
Fredric Neal Gabler
Richard Samuel Federick Gabrielle
James Andrew Gadiel
Pamela Lee Gaff
Ervin Vincent Gailliard
Deanna Lynn Galante
Grace Catherine Galante
Anthony Edward Gallagher
Daniel James Gallagher
John Patrick Gallagher
Lourdes Galletti
Cono E. Gallo
Vincenzo Gallucci
Thomas E. Galvin
Giovanna Galletta Gambale
Thomas Gambino, Jr.
Giann Franco Gamboa
Peter Ganci
Ladkat K. Ganesh
Claude Michael Gann
Osseni Garba
Charles William Garbarini
Ceasar Garcia
David Garcia
Juan Garcia
Marlyn Del Carmen Garcia
Christopher S. Gardner
Douglas Benjamin Gardner
Harvey J. Gardner III
Jeffrey Brian Gardner
Thomas Gardner
William Arthur Gardner
Francesco Garfi
Rocco Nino Gargano
James M. Gartenberg
Matthew David Garvey
Bruce Gary
Boyd Alan Gatton
Donald Richard Gavagan, Jr.
Terence D. Gazzani
Gary Geidel
Paul Hamilton Geier
Julie M. Geis

Peter G. Gelinas
Steven Paul Geller
Howard G. Gelling
Peter Victor Genco, Jr.
Steven Gregory Genovese
Alayne Gentul
Edward F. Geraghty
Suzanne Geraty
Ralph Gerhardt
Robert Gerlich
Denis P. Germain
Marina Romanovna Gertsberg
Susan M. Getzendanner
James G. Geyer
Joseph M. Giaccone
Vincent Francis Giammona
Debra Lynn Gibbon
James Andrew Giberson
Craig Neil Gibson
Ronnie E. Gies
Laura A. Giglio
Andrew Clive Gilbert
Timothy Paul Gilbert
Paul Stuart Gilbey
Paul John Gill
Mark Y. Gilles
Evan Gillette
Ronald Lawrence Gilligan
Rodney C. Gillis
Laura Gilly
John F. Ginley
Donna Marie Giordano
Jeffrey John Giordano
John Giordano
Steven A. Giorgetti
Martin Giovinazzo
Kum-Kum Girolamo
Salvatore Gitto
Cynthia Giugliano
Mon Gjonbalaj
Dianne Gladstone
Keith Glascoe
Thomas Irwin Glasser
Harry Glenn
Barry H. Glick
Steven Glick
John T. Gnazzo
William Robert Godshalk
Michael Gogliormella
Brian Fredric Goldberg
Jeffrey Grant Goldflam
Michelle Goldstein
Monica Goldstein
Steven Goldstein
Andrew H. Golkin
Dennis James Gomes
Enrique Antonio Gomez
Jose Bienvenido Gomez
Manuel Gomez, Jr.
Wilder Alfredo Gomez
Jenine Nicole Gonzalez

Mauricio Gonzalez
Rosa Gonzalez
Calvin J. Gooding
Harry Goody
Kiran Reddy Gopu
Catherine C. Gorayeb
Kerene Gordon
Sebastian Gorki
Kieran Joseph Gorman
Thomas Edward Gorman
Michael Edward Gould
Yuji Goya
Jon Richard Grabowski
Christopher Michael Grady
Edwin J. Graf III
David Martin Graifman
Gilbert Franco Granados
Elvira Granitto
Winston Arthur Grant
Christopher S. Gray
James Michael Gray
Tara McCloud Gray
Linda Catherine Grayling
John M. Grazioso
Timothy George Grazioso
Derrick Auther Green
Wade B. Green
Elaine Myra Greenberg
Gayle R. Greene
James Arthur Greenleaf, Jr.
Eileen Marsha Greenstein
Elizabeth Martin Gregg
Denise Gregory
Donald H. Gregory
Florence Moran Gregory
Pedro Grehan
John Michael Griffin
Tawanna Sherry Griffin
Joan Donna Griffith
Warren Grifka
Ramon Grijalvo
Joseph F. Grillo
David Joseph Grimner
Kenneth George Grouzalis
Joseph Grzelak
Matthew James Grzymalski
Robert Joseph Gschaar
Liming Gu
Jose Guadalupe
Cindy Yan Zhu Guan
Joel Guevara Gonzalez
Geoffrey E. Guja
Joseph Gullickson
Babita Girjamatie Guman
Douglas Brian Gurian
Janet Ruth Gustafson
Philip T. Guza
Barbara Guzzardo
Peter M. Gyulavary
Gary Robert Haag
Andrea Lyn Haberman

Barbara Mary Habib
Philip Haentzler
Nezam A. Hafiz
Karen Elizabeth Hagerty
Steven Michael Hagis
Mary Lou Hague
David Halderman
Maile Rachel Hale
Richard B. Hall
Vaswald George Hall
Robert J. Halligan
Vincent Gerard Halloran
James Douglas Halvorson
Mohammad Salman Hamdani
Felicia Hamilton
Robert Hamilton
Frederic K. Han
Christopher J. Hanley
Sean S. Hanley
Valerie Joan Hanna
Thomas Hannafin
Kevin James Hannaford
Michael Lawrence Hannan
Dana R Hannon
Vassilios G. Haramis
James A. Haran
Jeffrey Pike Hardy
Timothy John Hargrave
Daniel Edward Harlin
Frances Haros
Harvey Harrell
Stephen G. Harrell
Melissa Marie Harrington
Aisha Anne Harris
Stewart Dennis Harris
John Patrick Hart
John Clinton Hartz
Emeric Harvey
Thomas Theodore Haskell, Jr.
Timothy Haskell
Joseph John Hasson III
Leonard W. Hatton
Terence S. Hatton
Michael Haub
Timothy Aaron Haviland
Donald G. Havlish, Jr.
Anthony Hawkins
Nobuhiro Hayatsu
Philip Hayes
William Ward Haynes
Scott Jordan Hazelcorn
Michael K. Healey
Roberta B. Heber
Charles Francis Xavier Heeran
John F. Heffernan
H. Joseph Heller, Jr.
Joann L. Heltibridle
Mark F. Hemschoot
Ronnie Lee Henderson
Brian Hennessey
Michelle Marie Henrique

Joseph Henry
William Henry
John Christopher Henwood
Robert Allan Hepburn
Mary Herencia
Lindsay C. Herkness III
Harvey Robert Hermer
Claribel Hernandez
Eduardo Hernandez
Nuberto Hernandez
Raul Hernandez
Gary Herold
Jeffrey A. Hersch
Thomas Hetzel
Brian Hickey
Ysidro Hidalgo
Timothy Higgins
Robert D. W. Higley II
Todd Russell Hill
Clara Victorine Hinds
Neal O. Hinds
Mark D. Hindy
Katsuyuki Hirai
Heather Malia Ho
Tara Yvette Hobbs
Thomas Anderson Hobbs
James J. Hobin
Robert Wayne Hobson
DaJuan Hodges
Ronald George Hoerner
Patrick A. Hoey
Marcia Hoffman
Stephen G. Hoffman
Frederick Joseph Hoffmann
Michele L. Hoffmann
Judith Florence Hofmiller
Thomas Warren Hohlweck, Jr.
Jonathan R. Hohmann
John Holland
Joseph F. Holland
Elizabeth Holmes
Thomas Holohan
Bradley Hoorn
James P. Hopper
Montgomery McCullough Hord
Michael Horn
Matthew Douglas Horning
Robert L. Horohoe, Jr.
Aaron Horwitz
Charles Houston
Uhuru G. Houston
George Howard
Michael C. Howell
Steven Leon Howell
Jennifer L. Howley
Milagros Hromada
Marian R. Hrycak
Stephen Huczko, Jr.
Kris Robert Hughes
Paul Rexford Hughes
Robert Thomas Hughes

Thomas Hughes
Timothy Robert Hughes
Susan Huie
Lamar Hulse
William Christopher Hunt
Kathleen Anne Hunt-Casey
Joseph Hunter
Robert R. Hussa
Abid Hussain
Thomas Edward Hynes
Walter G. Hynes
Joseph Anthony Ianelli
Zuhtu Ibis
Jonathan Lee Ielpi
Michael Iken
Daniel Ilkanayev
Frederick Ill, Jr.
Abraham Nethanel Ilowitz
Anthony P. Infante, Jr.
Louis S. Inghilterra, Jr.
Christopher Noble Ingrassia
Paul Innella
Stephanie Veronica Irby
Douglas Irgang
Kristin A. Irvine Ryan
Todd Antione Isaac
Erik Isbrandtsen
Taizo Ishikawa
Aram Iskenderian, Jr.
John F. Iskyan
Kazushige Ito
Aleksandr Valeryevich Ivantsov
Virginia May Jablonski
Brooke Alexandra Jackman
Aaron Jeremy Jacobs
Ariel Louis Jacobs
Jason Kyle Jacobs
Michael Grady Jacobs
Steven A. Jacobson
Ricknauth Jaggernauth
Jake Denis Jagoda
Yudh Vir Singh Jain
Maria Jakubiak
Ernest James
Gricelda E. James
Priscilla James
Mark Steven Jardim
Muhammadou Jawara
Francois Jean-Pierre
Maxima Jean-Pierre
Paul Edward Jeffers
Alva Cynthia Jeffries Sanchez
Joseph Jenkins, Jr.
Alan Keith Jensen
Prem N. Jerath
Farah Jeudy
Hweidar Jian
Eliezer Jimenez, Jr.
Luis Jimenez, Jr.
Fernando Jimenez-Molina
Charles Gregory John

Nicholas John
LaShawna Johnson
Scott Michael Johnson
William R. Johnston
Allison Horstmann Jones
Arthur Joseph Jones
Brian Leander Jones
Christopher D. Jones
Donald T. Jones
Donald W. Jones
Linda Jones
Mary S. Jones
Andrew Jordan
Robert Thomas Jordan
Albert Gunnia Joseph
Guylene Joseph
Ingeborg Joseph
Karl Henry Joseph
Stephen Joseph
Jane Eileen Josiah
Anthony Jovic
Angel L. Juarbe, Jr.
Karen Sue Juday
Mychal F. Judge
Paul William Jurgens
Thomas Edward Jurgens
Kacinga Kabeya
Shashikiran Lakshmikantha Kadaba
Gavkharoy Kamardinova
Shari Kandell
Howard Lee Kane
Jennifer Lynn Kane
Vincent D. Kane
Joon Koo Kang
Sheldon Robert Kanter
Deborah H. Kaplan
Alvin Peter Kappelmann, Jr.
Charles Karczewski
William A. Karnes
Douglas Gene Karpiloff
Charles L. Kasper
Andrew K. Kates
John Katsimatides
Robert Michael Kaulfers
Don Jerome Kauth, Jr.
Hideya Kawauchi
Edward T. Keane
Richard M. Keane
Lisa Yvonne Kearney-Griffin
Karol Ann Keasler
Paul Hanlon Keating
Leo Russell Keene III
Joseph John Keller
Peter R. Kellerman
Joseph P. Kellett
Frederick H. Kelley, Jr.
James Joseph Kelly
Joseph A. Kelly
Maurice P. Kelly
Richard John Kelly, Jr.
Thomas Michael Kelly

Thomas Richard Kelly
Thomas W. Kelly
Timothy Colin Kelly
William Hill Kelly, Jr.
Robert Clinton Kennedy
Thomas J. Kennedy
John R. Keohane
Ronald T. Kerwin
Howard L. Kestenbaum
Douglas D. Ketcham
Ruth Ellen Ketler
Boris Khalif
Sarah Khan
Taimour Firaz Khan
Rajesh Khandelwal
Oliva Khemrat
SeiLai Khoo
Michael Kiefer
Satoshi Kikuchihara
Andrew Jay-Hoon Kim
Lawrence D. Kim
Mary Jo Kimelman
Andrew M. King
Lucille Teresa King
Robert King, Jr.
Lisa King-Johnson
Takashi Kinoshita
Chris Michael Kirby
Howard Barry Kirschbaum
Glenn Davis Kirwin
Helen Crossin Kittle
Richard Joseph Klares
Peter Anton Klein
Alan David Kleinberg
Karen Joyce Klitzman
Ronald Philip Kloepfer
Evgueni Kniazev
Andrew Knox
Thomas Patrick Knox
Rebecca Lee Koborie
Deborah A. Kobus
Gary Edward Koecheler
Frank J. Koestner
Ryan Kohart
Vanessa Kolpak
Irina Kolpakova
Suzanne Kondratenko
Abdoulaye Kone
Bon-Seok Koo
Dorota Kopiczko
Scott Kopytko
Bojan Kostic
Danielle Kousoulis
John J. Kren
William E. Krukowski
Lyudmila Ksido
Shekhar Kumar
Kenneth Kumpel
Frederick Kuo, Jr.
Patricia Kuras
Nauka Kushitani

Thomas Kuveikis
Victor Kwarkye
Kui Fai Kwok
Angela Reed Kyte
Andrew La Corte
Amarnauth Lachhman
James Patrick Ladley
Joseph A. LaFalce
Jeanette Louise Lafond-Menichino
David Laforge
Michael Laforte
Alan Charles LaFrance
Juan Lafuente
Neil Kwong-Wah Lai
Vincent Anthony Laieta
William David Lake
Franco Lalama
Chow Kwan Lam
Stephen LaMantia
Amy Hope Lamonsoff
Nickola Lampley
Robert Lane
Brendan Mark Lang
Rosanne P. Lang
Vanessa Langer
Mary Louise Langley
Peter J. Langone
Thomas Michael Langone
Michele Bernadette Lanza
Ruth Sheila Lapin
Carol Ann LaPlante
Ingeborg Lariby
Robin Blair Larkey
Christopher Randall Larrabee
Hamidou S. Larry
Scott Larsen
John Adam Larson
Gary Edward Lasko
Nicholas Craig Lassman
Paul Laszczynski
Jeffrey G. LaTouche
Charles Laurencin
Stephen James Lauria
Maria LaVache
Denis Francis Lavelle
Jeannine Mary LaVerde
Anna A. Laverty
Steven Lawn
Robert Lawrence
Nathaniel Lawson
Eugen Gabriel Lazar
James Patrick Leahy
Joseph Gerard Leavey
Neil Joseph Leavy
Leon Lebor
Kenneth Charles Ledee
Alan J. Lederman
Elena F. Ledesma
Alexis Leduc
David S. Lee
Gary H. Lee

Hyun Joon Lee
Juanita Lee
Kathryn Blair Lee
Linda C. Lee
Lorraine Mary Lee
Myoung Woo Lee
Richard Y. Lee
Stuart Soo-Jin Lee
Yang Der Lee
Stephen Paul Lefkowitz
Adriana Legro
Edward Joseph Lehman
Eric Andrew Lehrfeld
David Leistman
David Prudencio Lemagne
Joseph Anthony Lenihan
John Joseph Lennon, Jr.
John Robinson Lenoir
Jorge Luis Leon
Matthew Gerard Leonard
Michael Lepore
Charles A. Lesperance
Jeff Leveen
John Dennis Levi
Alisha Caren Levin
Neil David Levin
Robert Levine
Robert Michael Levine
Shai Levinhar
Adam Jay Lewis
Margaret Susan Lewis
Ye Wei Liang
Orasri Liangthanasarn
Daniel F. Libretti
Ralph Licciardi
Edward Lichtschein
Steven Barry Lillianthal
Carlos R. Lillo
Craig Damian Lilore
Arnold A. Lim
Darya Lin
Wei Rong Lin
Nickie L. Lindo
Thomas V. Linehan, Jr.
Robert Thomas Linnane
Alan P. Linton, Jr.
Diane Theresa Lipari
Kenneth Lira
Francisco Alberto Liriano
Lorraine Lisi
Paul Lisson
Vincent M. Litto
Ming-Hao Liu
Nancy Liz
Harold Lizcano
Martin Lizzul
George A. Llanes
Elizabeth C. Logler
Catherine Lisa Loguidice
Jerome Robert Lohez
Michael William Lomax

Laura Maria Longing
Salvatore Lopes
Daniel Lopez
George Lopez
Luis Manuel Lopez
Manuel L. Lopez
Joseph Lostrangio
Chet Dek Louie
Stuart Seid Louis
Joseph Lovero
Jenny Seu Kueng Low Wong
Michael W. Lowe
Garry W. Lozier
John Peter Lozowsky
Charles Peter Lucania
Edward Hobbs Luckett
Mark Gavin Ludvigsen
Lee Charles Ludwig
Sean Thomas Lugano
Daniel Lugo
Marie Lukas
William Lum, Jr.
Michael P. Lunden
Christopher Lunder
Anthony Luparello
Gary Frederick Lutnick
William Lutz
Linda Anne Luzzicone
Alexander Lygin
Farrell Peter Lynch
James Francis Lynch
Louise A. Lynch
Michael Cameron Lynch
Michael F. Lynch
Michael Francis Lynch
Richard D. Lynch, Jr.
Robert Henry Lynch, Jr.
Sean P. Lynch
Sean Patrick Lynch
Michael J. Lyons
Monica Anne Lyons
Patrick Lyons
Robert Francis Mace
Jan Maciejewski
Catherine Fairfax Macrae
Richard Blaine Madden
Simon Maddison Noell Maerz
Jennieann Maffeo
Joseph Maffeo
Jay Robert Magazine
Brian Magee
Charles Wilson Magee
Joseph V. Maggitti
Ronald Magnuson
Daniel L. Maher
Thomas Anthony Mahon
William J. Mahoney
Joseph Daniel Maio
Takashi Makimoto
Abdu Ali Malahi
Debora I. Maldonado

Myrna T. Maldonado-Agosto
Alfred Russell Maler
Gregory James Malone
Edward Francis Maloney III
Joseph Maloney
Gene Edward Maloy
Christian Maltby
Francisco Miguel Mancini
Joseph Mangano
Sara Elizabeth Manley
Debra Mannetta
Marion Victoria Manning
Terence John Manning
James Maounis
Joseph Ross Marchbanks, Jr.
Peter Edward Mardikian
Edward Joseph Mardovich
Charles Joseph Margiotta
Kenneth Joseph Marino
Lester V. Marino
Vita Marino
Kevin Marlo
Jose Marrero
John Marshall
James Martello
Michael A. Marti
Peter C. Martin
William J. Martin, Jr.
Brian E. Martineau
Betsy Martinez
Edward Martinez
Jose Angel Martinez, Jr.
Robert Gabriel Martinez
Victor Martinez Pastrana
Lizie D. Martinez-Calderon
Paul Richard Martini
Joseph A. Mascali
Bernard Mascarenhas
Stephen Frank Masi
Nicholas George Massa
Patricia Ann Massari
Michael Massaroli
Philip William Mastrandrea, Jr.
Rudolph Mastrocinque
Joseph Mathai
Charles Mathers
William A. Mathesen
Marcello Matricciano
Margaret Elaine Mattic
Robert D. Mattson
Walter Matuza
Charles A. Mauro, Jr.
Charles J. Mauro
Dorothy Mauro
Nancy T. Mauro
Tyrone May
Keithroy Marcellus Maynard
Robert J. Mayo
Kathy Nancy Mazza
Edward Mazzella, Jr.
Jennifer Lynn Mazzotta

Kaaria Mbaya
James Joseph McAlary
Brian McAleese
Patricia Ann McAneney
Colin Robert McArthur
John Kevin McAvoy
Kenneth M. McBrayer
Brendan McCabe
Micheal McCabe
Thomas McCann
Justin McCarthy
Kevin M. McCarthy
Michael McCarthy
Robert McCarthy
Stanley McCaskill
Katie Marie McCloskey
Joan McConnell-Cullinan
Charles Austin McCrann
Tonyell F. McDay
Matthew T. McDermott
Joseph P. McDonald
Brian Grady McDonnell
Michael P. McDonnell
John McDowell, Jr.
Eamon J. McEneaney
John Thomas McErlean, Jr.
Daniel Francis McGinley
Mark Ryan McGinly
William E. McGinn
Thomas Henry MCGinnis
Michael Gregory McGinty
Ann McGovern
Scott Martin McGovern
William McGovern
Stacey Sennas McGowan
Francis Noel McGuinn
Patrick McGuire
Thomas M. McHale
Keith McHeffey
Ann M. McHugh
Denis J. McHugh III
Dennis McHugh
Michael E. McHugh
Robert G. McIlvaine
Donald James McIntyre
Stephanie Marie McKenna
Barry J. McKeon
Evelyn C. McKinnedy
Darryl Leron McKinney
George Patrick McLaughlin, Jr.
Robert C. McLaughlin, Jr.
Gavin McMahon
Robert D. McMahon
Edmund McNally
Daniel W. McNeal
Walter Arthur McNeil
Jisley McNish
Christine Sheila McNulty
Sean Peter McNulty
Robert McPadden
Terence A. McShane

Timothy Patrick McSweeney
Martin E. McWilliams
Rocco A. Medaglia
Abigail Cales Medina
Ana Iris Medina
Deborah Louise Medwig
Damian Meehan
William J. Meehan
Alok Mehta
Raymond Meisenheimer
Manuel Emilio Mejia
Eskedar Melaku
Antonio Melendez
Mary Melendez
Yelena Melnichenko
Stuart Todd Meltzer
Diarelia Jovanah Mena
Charles Mendez
Lizette Mendoza
Shevonne Olicia Mentis
Steven Mercado
Westly Mercer
Ralph Joseph Mercurio
Alan Harvey Merdinger
George L. Merino
Yamel Merino
George Merkouris
Deborah Merrick
Raymond Joseph Metz III
Jill Ann Metzler
David Robert Meyer
Nurul H. Miah
William Edward Micciulli
Martin Paul Michelstein
Peter Teague Milano
Gregory Milanowycz
Lukasz Tomasz Milewski
Sharon Christina Millan
Corey Peter Miller
Craig James Miller
Douglas Charles Miller
Henry Alfred Miller, Jr.
Joel Miller
Michael Matthew Miller
Philip D. Miller
Robert Alan Miller
Robert Cromwell Miller, Jr.
Benjamin Millman
Charles Morris Mills
Ronald Keith Milstein
Robert Minara
William George Minardi
Diakite Minata
Louis Joseph Minervino
Thomas Mingione
Wilbert Miraille
Dominick N. Mircovich
Rajesh Arjan Mirpuri
Joseph Mistrulli
Susan J. Miszkowicz
Paul Thomas Mitchell

Richard P. Miuccio
Frank V. Moccia, Sr.
Louis Joseph Modafferi
Boyie Mohammed
Dennis Mojica
Manuel Mojica
Kleber Molina
Manuel De Jesus Molina
Carl Molinaro
Justin Molisani
Brian Monaghan
Franklin Monahan
John Monahan
Kristen Montanaro
Craig Montano
Michael Montesi
Jeffrey Montgomery
Peter Montoulieu
Cheryl Ann Monyak
Thomas Moody
Sharon Moore
Krishna Moorthy
Abner Morales
Carlos Manuel Morales
Luis Morales
Paula E. Morales John Moran
John Chrisopher Moran
Kathleen Moran
Lindsay Stapleton Morehouse
George Morell
Steven P. Morello
Vincent S. Morello
Yvette Nicole Moreno
Dorothy Morgan
Richard Morgan
Nancy Morgenstern
Sanae Mori
Blanca Robertina Morocho
Leonel Geronimo Morocho
Dennis Gerard Moroney
Lynne Irene Morris
Seth Allan Morris
Stephen Philip Morris
Christopher Martel Morrison
Jorge Luis Morron Garcia
Ferdinand V. Morrone
William David Moskal
Marco Motroni
Cynthia Motus-Wilson
Iouri A. Mouchinski
Jude Joseph Moussa
Peter Moutos
Damion O'Neil Mowatt
Christopher Mozzillo
Stephen Vincent Mulderry
Richard Muldowney Jr
Michael D. Mullan
Dennis Michael Mulligan
Peter James Mulligan
Michael Joseph Mullin
James Donald Munhall

Nancy Muniz
Carlos Munoz
Frank Munoz
Theresa Munson
Robert M. Murach
Cesar Augusto Murillo
Marc A. Murolo
Brian Joseph Murphy
Charles Anthony Murphy
Christopher W. Murphy
Edward Charles Murphy
James F. Murphy Iv
James Thomas Murphy
Kevin James Murphy
Patrick Sean Murphy
Raymond E. Murphy
Robert Eddie Murphy, Jr.
John Joseph Murray
John Joseph Murray, Jr.
Susan D. Murray
Valerie Victoria Murray
Richard Todd Myhre
Robert B. Nagel
Takuya Nakamura
Alexander Napier
Frank Joseph Naples III
John Napolitano
Catherine Ann Nardella
Mario Nardone, Jr.
Manika K. Narula
Mehmood Naseem
Narender Nath
Karen Susan Navarro
Joseph Micheal Navas
Francis Joseph Nazario
Glenroy I. Neblett
Rayman Marcus Neblett
Jerome O. Nedd
Laurence Nedell
Luke G. Nee
Pete Negron
Ann N. Nelson
David William Nelson
James Nelson
Michele Ann Nelson
Peter Allen Nelson
Oscar Francis Nesbitt
Gerard Terence Nevins
Christopher Newton-Carter
Kapinga Ngalula
Nancy Yuen Ngo
Jody Nichilo
Martin S. Niederer
Alfonse Joseph Niedermeyer
Frank John Niestadt, Jr.
Gloria Nieves
Juan Nieves, Jr.
Troy Edward Nilsen
Paul Nimbley
John B. Niven
Katherine Marie Noack

Curtis Terrance Noel
Daniel R. Nolan
Robert Noonan
Daniela R. Notaro
Brian Christopher Novotny
Soichi Numata
Brian Felix Nunez
Jose Nunez
Jeffrey Roger Nussbaum
Dennis O'Berg
James P. O'Brien, Jr.
Michael P. O'Brien
Scott J. O'Brien
Timothy Michael O'Brien
Daniel O'Callaghan
Dennis James O'Connor, Jr.
Diana J. O'Connor
Keith Kevin O'Connor
Richard J. O'Connor
Amy O'Doherty
Marni Pont O'Doherty
James Andrew O'Grady
Thomas O'Hagan
Patrick J. O'Keefe
William O'Keefe
Gerald O'leary
Matthew Timothy O'Mahony
Peter J. O'Neill, Jr.
Sean Gordon O'Neill
Kevin O'Rourke
Patrick J. O'Shea
Robert William O'Shea
Timothy F. O'Sullivan
James A. Oakley
Douglas E. Oelschlager
Takashi Ogawa
Albert Ogletree
Philip Paul Ognibene
Joseph J. Ogren
Samuel Oitice
Gerald Michael Olcott
Christine Anne Olender
Linda Mary Oliva
Edward Kraft Oliver
Leah E. Oliver
Eric T. Olsen
Jeffrey James Olsen
Maureen Lyons Olson
Steven John Olson
Toshihiro Onda
Seamus L. O'Neal
John P. Oneill
Frank Oni
Michael C. Opperman
Christopher Orgielewicz
Margaret Orloske
Virginia Anne Ormiston
Ronald Orsini
Peter Ortale
Juan Ortega-Campos
Alexander Ortiz

David Ortiz
Emilio Ortiz, Jr.
Pablo Ortiz
Paul Ortiz, Jr.
Sonia Ortiz
Masaru Ose
Elsy C. Osorio
James R. Ostrowski
Jason Douglas Oswald
Michael Otten
Isidro D. Ottenwalder
Michael Chung Ou
Todd Joseph Ouida
Jesus Ovalles
Peter J. Owens, Jr.
Adianes Oyola
Angel M. Pabon
Israel Pabon, Jr.
Roland Pacheco
Michael Benjamin Packer
Rene Padilla-Chavarria
Deepa Pakkala
Jeffrey Matthew Palazzo
Thomas Palazzo
Richard Palazzolo
Orio J. Palmer
Frank Anthony Palombo
Alan N. Palumbo
Christopher Matthew Panatier
Dominique Lisa Pandolfo
Paul J. Pansini
John M. Paolillo
Edward Joseph Papa
Salvatore T. Papasso
James Nicholas Pappageorge
Vinod Kumar Parakat
Vijayashanker Paramsothy
Nitin Parandkar
Hardai Parbhu
James Wendell Parham
Debra Marie Paris
George Paris
Gye Hyong Park
Philip Lacey Parker
Michael Alaine Parkes
Robert E. Parks, Jr.
Hashmukhrai C. Parmar
Robert Parro
Diane Marie Parsons
Leobardo Lopez Pascual
Michael Pascuma
Jerrold Paskins
Horace Robert Passananti
Suzanne H. Passaro
Avnish Ramanbhai Patel
Dipti Patel
Manish Patel
Steven Bennett Paterson
James Matthew Patrick
Manuel D. Patrocino
Bernard E. Patterson

Cira Marie Patti
Robert E. Pattison
James Robert Paul
Patrice Paz
Victor Paz-Gutierrez
Stacey Lynn Peak
Richard Allen Pearlman
Durrell V. Pearsall
Thomas Pedicini
Todd Douglas Pelino
Michel Adrian Pelletier
Anthony G. Peluso
Angel Ramon Pena
Richard Al Penny
Salvatore F. Pepe
Carl Peralta
Robert David Peraza
Jon A. Perconti
Alejo Perez
Angel Perez, Jr.
Angela Susan Perez
Anthony Perez
Ivan Perez
Nancy E. Perez
Joseph John Perroncino
Edward J. Perrotta
Emelda H. Perry
Glenn C. Perry
John William Perry
Franklin Allan Pershep
Danny Pesce
Michael John Pescherine
Davin Peterson
William Russell Peterson
Mark Petrocelli
Philip Scott Petti
Glen Kerrin Pettit
Dominick Pezzulo
Kaleen Elizabeth Pezzuti
Kevin Pfeifer
Tu-Anh Pham
Kenneth Phelan
Sneha Ann Philips
Gerard Phillips
Suzette Eugenia Piantieri
Ludwig John Picarro
Matthew M. Picerno
Joseph Oswald Pick
Christopher Pickford
Dennis J. Pierce
Bernard Pietronico
Nicholas P. Pietrunti
Theodoros Pigis
Susan Elizabeth Pinto
Joseph Piskadlo
Christopher Todd Pitman
Joshua Piver
Joseph Plumitallo
John Pocher
William Howard Pohlmann
Laurence Polatsch

Thomas H. Polhemus
Steve Pollicino
Susan M. Pollio
Joshua Iousa Poptean
Giovanna Porras
Anthony Portillo
James Edward Potorti
Daphne Pouletsos
Richard N. Poulos
Stephen Emanual Poulos
Brandon Jerome Powell
Shawn Edward Powell
Antonio Pratt
Gregory M. Preziose
Wanda Ivelisse Prince
Vincent Princiotta
Kevin Prior
Everett Martin Proctor III
Carrie Beth Progen
Sarah Prothero-Redheffer
David Lee Pruim
Richard Prunty
John Foster Puckett
Robert David Pugliese
Edward F. Pullis
Patricia Ann Puma
Hemanth Kumar Puttur
Edward R. Pykon
Christopher Quackenbush
Lars Peter Qualben
Lincoln Quappe
Beth Ann Quigley
Michael Quilty
James Francis Quinn
Ricardo J. Quinn
Carlos Quishpe-Cuaman
Carol Millicent Rabalais
Christopher Peter A. Racaniello
Leonard J. Ragaglia
Eugene Raggio
Laura Marie Ragonese-Snik
Michael Ragusa
Peter Frank Raimondi
Harry A. Raines
Ehtesham Raja
Valsa Raju
Edward Rall
Lukas Rambousek
Maria Ramirez
Harry Ramos
Vishnoo Ramsaroop
Lorenzo E. Ramzey
Alfred Todd Rancke
Adam David Rand
Jonathan C. Randall
Srinivasa Shreyas Ranganath
Anne T. Ransom
Faina Aronovna Rapoport
Robert A. Rasmussen
Amenia Rasool
Roger Mark Rasweiler

David Alan Rathkey
William Ralph Raub
Gerard P. Rauzi
Alexey Razuvaev
Gregory Reda
Michele Reed
Judith Ann Reese
Donald J. Regan
Robert M. Regan
Thomas Michael Regan
Christian Michael Otto Regenhard
Howard Reich
Gregg Reidy
James Brian Reilly
Kevin O. Reilly
Timothy E. Reilly
Joseph Reina, Jr.
Thomas Barnes Reinig
Frank Bennett Reisman
Joshua Scott Reiss
Karen Renda
John Armand Reo
Richard Cyril Rescorla
John Thomas Resta
Luis Clodoaldo Revilla
Eduvigis Reyes, Jr.
Bruce Albert Reynolds
John Frederick Rhodes
Francis Saverio Riccardelli
Rudolph N. Riccio
Ann Marie Riccoboni
David H. Rice
Eileen Mary Rice
Kenneth Frederick Rice III
Vernon Allan Richard
Claude Daniel Richards
Gregory David Richards
Michael Richards
Venesha Orintia Richards
James C. Riches
Alan Jay Richman
John M. Rigo
Theresa Risco
Rose Mary Riso
Moises N. Rivas
Joseph Rivelli
Carmen Alicia Rivera
Isaias Rivera
Juan William Rivera
Linda Ivelisse Rivera
David E. Rivers
Joseph R. Riverso
Paul V. Rizza
John Frank Rizzo
Stephen Louis Roach
Joseph Roberto
Leo Arthur Roberts
Michael Roberts
Michael Edward Roberts
Donald Walter Robertson, Jr.
Catherina Robinson

Jeffery Robinson
Michell Lee Jean Robotham
Donald A. Robson
Antonio A. Rocha
Raymond James Rocha
Laura Rockefeller
John Rodak
Antonio J. Rodrigues
Anthony Rodriguez
Carmen Milagros Rodriguez
Gregory Ernesto Rodriguez
Marsha A. Rodriguez
Mayra Valdes Rodriguez
Richard Rodriguez
David Bartolo Rodriguez-Vargas
Matthew Rogan
Karlie Barbara Rogers
Scott Williams Rohner
Keith Roma
Joseph M. Romagnolo
Efrain Romero, Sr.
Elvin Romero
Juan Romero
Orozco James A. Romito
Sean Paul Rooney
Eric Thomas Ropiteau
Aida Rosario
Angela Rosario
Wendy Alice Rosario Wakeford
Mark Rosen
Brooke David Rosenbaum
Linda Rosenbaum
Sheryl Lynn Rosenbaum
Lloyd Daniel Rosenberg
Mark Louis Rosenberg
Andrew Ira Rosenblum
Joshua M. Rosenblum
Joshua Alan Rosenthal
Richard David Rosenthal
Daniel Rosetti
Norman S. Rossinow
Nicholas P. Rossomando
Michael Craig Rothberg
Donna Marie Rothenberg
Nicholas Rowe
Timothy Alan Roy, Sr.
Paul G. Ruback
Ronald J. Ruben
Joanne Rubino
David M. Ruddle
Bart Joseph Ruggiere
Susan A. Ruggiero
Adam Keith Ruhalter
Gilbert Ruiz
Obdulio Ruiz Diaz
Stephen P. Russell
Steven Harris Russin
Michael Thomas Russo, Sr.
Wayne Alan Russo
Edward Ryan
John Joseph Ryan, Jr.

Jonathan Stephan Ryan
Matthew Lancelot Ryan
Tatiana Ryjova
Christina Sunga Ryook
Thierry Saada
Jason Elazar Sabbag
Thomas E. Sabella
Scott Saber
Joseph Francis Sacerdote
Neeraha Sadaranghani
Mohammad Ali Sadeque
Francis John Sadocha
Jude Safi
Brock Joel Safronoff
Edward Saiya
John Patrick Salamone
Hernando Salas
Juan G. Salas
Esmerlin Antonio Salcedo
John Salvatore Salerno, Jr.
Richard L. Salinardi, Jr.
Wayne John Saloman
Nolbert Salomon
Catherine Patricia Salter
Frank Salvaterra
Paul Richard Salvio
Samuel Robert Salvo, Jr.
Rena Sam-Dinnoo
Carlos Alberto Samaniego
James Kenneth Samuel, Jr.
Michael San Phillip
Sylvia San Pio
Hugo M. Sanay
Erick Sanchez
Jacquelyn Patrice Sanchez
Eric M. Sand
Stacey Leigh Sanders
Herman S. Sandler
James Sands, Jr.
Ayleen J. Santiago
Kirsten Santiago
Maria Theresa Santillan
Susan Gayle Santo
Christopher Santora
John A. Santore
Mario L. Santoro
Rafael Humberto Santos
Rufino Conrado Flores Santos Iii
Jorge Octavio Santos Anaya
Kalyan Sarkar
Chapelle R. Sarker
Paul F. Sarle
Deepika Kumar Sattaluri
Gregory Thomas Saucedo
Susan M. Sauer
Anthony Savas
Vladimir Savinkin
Jackie Sayegh
John Michael Sbarbaro
Robert L. Scandole, Jr.
Michelle Scarpitta

Dennis Scauso
John Albert Schardt
John G. Scharf
Frederick Claude Scheffold, Jr.
Angela Susan Scheinberg
Scott Mitchell Schertzer
Sean Schielke
Steven Francis Schlag
Jon Schlissel
Karen Helene Schmidt
Ian Schneider
Thomas G. Schoales
Frank G. Schott, Jr.
Gerard Patrick Schrang
Jeffrey H. Schreier
John T. Schroeder
Susan Lee Schuler
Edward William Schunk
Mark E. Schurmeier
Clarin Shellie Schwartz
John Burkhart Schwartz
Mark Schwartz
Adriane Victoria Scibetta
Raphael Scorca
Randolph Scott
Sheila Scott
Christopher Jay Scudder
Arthur Warren Scullin
Michael Herman Seaman
Margaret M. Seeliger
Anthony Segarra
Carlos Segarra
Jason Sekzer
Matthew Carmen Sellitto
Howard Selwyn
Larry John Senko
Arturo Angelo Sereno
Frankie Serrano
Alena Sesinova
Adele Christine Sessa
Sita Nermalla Sewnarine
Karen Lynn Seymour
Davis Sezna
Thomas Joseph Sgroi
Jayesh S. Shah
Khalid M. Shahid
Mohammed Shajahan
Gary Shamay
Earl Richard Shanahan
Neil Shastri
Kathryn Anne Shatzoff
Barbara A. Shaw
Jeffrey James Shaw
Robert John Shay, Jr.
Daniel James Shea
Joseph Patrick Shea
Linda Sheehan
Hagay Shefi
John Anthony Sherry
Atsushi Shiratori
Thomas Joseph Shubert
Mark Shulman
See Wong Shum
Allan Abraham Shwartzstein
Johanna Sigmund
Dianne T. Signer
Gregory Sikorsky
Stephen Gerard Siller
David Silver
Craig A. Silverstein
Nasima Hameed Simjee
Bruce Edward Simmons
Arthur Simon
Kenneth Alan Simon
Michael J. Simon
Paul Joseph Simon
Marianne Teresa Simone
Barry Simowitz
Jeff Lyal Simpson
Khamladai Singh
Kulwant Singh
Roshan Ramesh Singh
Thomas E. Sinton III
Peter A. Siracuse
Muriel Fay Siskopoulos
Joseph Michael Sisolak
John P. Skala
Francis Joseph Skidmore, Jr.
Toyena Skinner
Paul A. Skrzypek
Christopher Paul Slattery
Vincent Robert Slavin
Robert F. Sliwak
Paul K. Sloan
Stanley S. Smagala, Jr.
Wendy L. Small
Catherine Smith
Daniel Laurence Smith
George Eric Smith
James Gregory Smith
Jeffrey R. Smith
Joyce Patricia Smith
Karl T. Smith
Keisha Smith
Kevin Joseph Smith
Leon Smith, Jr.
Moira Ann Smith
Rosemary A. Smith
Bonnie Jeanne Smithwick
Rochelle Monique Snell
Leonard J. Snyder, Jr.
Astrid Elizabeth Sohan
Sushil S. Solanki
Ruben Solares
Naomi Leah Solomon
Daniel W. Song
Michael Charles Sorresse
Fabian Soto
Timothy Patrick Soulas
Gregory Spagnoletti
Donald F. Spampinato, Jr.
Thomas Sparacio
John Anthony Spataro
Robert W. Spear, Jr.
Maynard S. Spence, Jr.
George Edward Spencer III
Robert Andrew Spencer
Mary Rubina Sperando
Tina Spicer
Frank Spinelli
William E. Spitz
Joseph Spor, Jr.
Klaus Johannes Sprockamp
Saranya Srinuan
Fitzroy St. Rose
Michael F. Stabile
Lawrence T. Stack
Timothy M. Stackpole
Richard James Stadelberger
Eric Stahlman
Gregory Stajk
Alexandru Liviu Stan
Corina Stan
Mary Domenica Stanley
Anthony Starita
Jeffrey Stark
Derek James Statkevicus
Craig William Staub
William V. Steckman
Eric Thomas Steen
William R. Steiner
Alexander Steinman
Andrew Stergiopoulos
Andrew Stern
Martha Stevens
Michael James Stewart
Richard H. Stewart, Jr.
Sanford M. Stoller
Lonny Jay Stone
Jimmy Nevill Storey
Timothy Stout
Thomas Strada
James J. Straine, Jr.
Edward W. Straub
George J. Strauch, Jr.
Edward T. Strauss
Steven R. Strauss
Steven F. Strobert
Walwyn W. Stuart, Jr.
Benjamin Suarez
David Scott Suarez
Ramon Suarez
Yoichi Sugiyama
William Christopher Sugra
Daniel Suhr
David Marc Sullins
Christopher P. Sullivan
Patrick Sullivan
Thomas Sullivan
Hilario Soriano Sumaya, Jr.
James Joseph Suozzo
Colleen Supinski
Robert Sutcliffe

Seline Sutter
Claudia Suzette Sutton
John Francis Swaine
Kristine M. Swearson
Brian Edward Sweeney
Kenneth J. Swenson
Thomas Swift
Derek Ogilvie Sword
Kevin Thomas Szocik
Gina Sztejnberg
Norbert P. Szurkowski
Harry Taback
Joann Tabeek
Norma C. Taddei
Michael Taddonio
Keiichiro Takahashi
Keiji Takahashi
Phyllis Gail Talbot
Robert Talhami
Sean Patrick Tallon
Paul Talty
Maurita Tam
Rachel Tamares
Hector Tamayo
Michael Andrew Tamuccio
Kenichiro Tanaka
Rhondelle Cheri Tankard
Michael Anthony Tanner
Dennis Gerard Taormina, Jr.
Kenneth Joseph Tarantino
Allan Tarasiewicz
Ronald Tartaro
Darryl Anthony Taylor
Donnie Brooks Taylor
Lorisa Ceylon Taylor
Michael Morgan Taylor
Paul A. Tegtmeier
Yeshauant Tembe
Anthony Tempesta
Dorothy Pearl Temple
Stanley Temple
David Tengelin
Brian John Terrenzi
Lisa M. Terry
Shell Tester
Goumatie T. Thackurdeen
Sumati Thakur
Harshad Sham Thatte
Thomas F. Theurkauf, Jr.
Lesley Anne Thomas
Brian Thomas Thompson
Clive Thompson
Glenn Thompson
Nigel Bruce Thompson
Perry A. Thompson
Vanavah Alexei Thompson
William H. Thompson
Eric Raymond Thorpe
Nichola Angela Thorpe
Sal Edward Tieri, Jr.
John p Tierney

Mary Ellen Tiesi
William R. Tieste
Kenneth Francis Tietjen
Stephen Edward Tighe
Scott Charles Timmes
Michael E. Tinley
Jennifer M. Tino
Robert Frank Tipaldi
John James Tipping II
David Tirado
Hector Luis Tirado, Jr.
Michelle Lee Titolo
John J. Tobin
Richard Todisco
Vladimir Tomasevic
Stephen Kevin Tompsett
Thomas Tong
Doris Torres
Luis Eduardo Torres
Amy Elizabeth Toyen
Christopher Michael Traina
Daniel Patrick Trant
Abdoul Karim Traore
Glenn J. Travers
Walter Philip Travers
Felicia Y. Traylor-Bass
Lisa L. Trerotola
Karamo Trerra
Michael Angel Trinidad
Francis Joseph Trombino
Gregory James Trost
William P. Tselepis
Zhanetta Valentinovna Tsoy
Michael Tucker
Lance Richard Tumulty
Ching Ping Tung
Simon James Turner
Donald Joseph Tuzio
Robert T. Twomey
Jennifer Tzemis
John G. Ueltzhoeffer
Tyler V. Ugolyn
Michael A. Uliano
Jonathan J. Uman
Anil Shivhari Umarkar
Allen V. Upton
Diane Marie Urban
John Damien Vaccacio
Bradley Hodges Vadas
Renuta Vaidea
William Valcarcel
Felix Antonio Vale
Ivan Vale
Benito Valentin
Santos Valentin, Jr.
Carlton Francis Valvo II
Erica H. Van Acker
Kenneth W. Van Auken
Richard B. Van Hine
Daniel M. Van Laere
Edward Raymond Vanacore

Jon C. Vandevander
Barrett Vanvelzer, 4
Edward Vanvelzer
Paul Herman Vanvelzer
Frederick Thomas Varacchi
Gopalakrishnan Varadhan
David Vargas
Scott C. Vasel
Azael Ismael Vasquez
Arcangel Vazquez
Santos Vazquez
Peter Anthony Vega
Sankara S. Velamuri
Jorge Velazquez
Lawrence G. Veling
Anthony Mark Ventura
David Vera
Loretta Ann Vero
Christopher James Vialonga
Matthew Gilbert Vianna
Robert Anthony Vicario
Celeste Torres Victoria
Joanna Vidal
John T. Vigiano II
Joseph Vincent Vigiano
Frank J. Vignola, Jr.
Joseph Barry Vilardo
Sergio Villanueva
Chantal Vincelli
Melissa Vincent
Francine Ann Virgilio
Lawrence Virgilio
Joseph Gerard Visciano
Joshua S. Vitale
Maria Percoco Vola
Lynette D. Vosges
Garo H. Voskerijian
Alfred Vukosa
Gregory Kamal Bruno Wachtler
Gabriela Waisman
Courtney Wainsworth Walcott
Victor Wald
Benjamin James Walker
Glen Wall
Mitchel Scott Wallace
Peter Guyder Wallace
Robert Francis Wallace
Roy Michael Wallace
Jeanmarie Wallendorf
Matthew Blake Wallens
John Wallice, Jr.
Barbara P. Walsh
James Henry Walsh
Jeffrey P. Walz
Ching Wang
Weibin Wang
Michael Warchola
Stephen Gordon Ward
James Arthur Waring
Brian G. Warner
Derrick Washington

Charles Waters
James Thomas Waters, Jr.
Patrick J. Waters
Kenneth Thomas Watson
Michael Henry Waye
Todd Christopher Weaver
Walter Edward Weaver
Nathaniel Webb
Dinah Webster
Joanne Flora Weil
Michael T. Weinberg
Steven Weinberg
Scott Jeffrey Weingard
Steven George Weinstein
Simon Weiser
David M. Weiss
David Thomas Weiss
Vincent Michael Wells
Timothy Matthew Welty
Christian Hans Rudolf Wemmers
Ssu-Hui Wen
Oleh D. Wengerchuk
Peter M. West
Whitfield West, Jr.
Meredith Lynn Whalen
Eugene Whelan
Adam S. White
Edward James White III
James Patrick White
John Sylvester White
Kenneth Wilburn White, Jr.
Leonard Anthony White
Malissa Y. White
Wayne White
Leanne Marie Whiteside
Mark P. Whitford
Michael T. Wholey
Mary Catherine Wieman
Jeffrey David Wiener
Wilham J. Wik
Alison Marie Wildman
Glenn E. Wilkenson
John C. Willett
Brian Patrick Williams
Crossley Richard Williams, Jr.
David J. Williams
Deborah Lynn Williams
Kevin Michael Williams
Louie Anthony Williams
Louis Calvin Williams III
John P. Williamson
Donna Ann Wilson
William Wilson
David Harold Winton
Glenn J. Winuk
Thomas Francis Wise
Alan L. Wisniewski
Frank Thomas Wisniewski
David Wiswall
Sigrid Wiswe
Michael Wittenstein

Christopher W. Wodenshek
Martin P. Wohlforth
Katherine Susan Wolf
Jennifer Yen Wong
Siu Cheung Wong
Yin Ping Wong
Yuk Ping Wong
Brent James Woodall
James John Woods
Patrick J. Woods
Richard Herron Woodwell
David Terence Wooley
John Bentley Works
Martin Michael Wortley
Rodney James Wotton
William Wren
John Wayne Wright
Neil Robin Wright
Sandra Lee Wright
Jupiter Yambem
Suresh Yanamadala
Matthew David Yarnell
Myrna Yaskulka
Shakila Yasmin
Olabisi Shadie Layeni Yee
William Yemele
Edward P. York
Kevin Patrick York
Raymond R. York
Suzanne Youmans
Barrington Young
Jacqueline Young
Elkin Yuen
Joseph C. Zaccoli
Adel Agayby Zakhary
Arkady Zaltsman
Edwin J. Zambrana, Jr.
Robert Alan Zampieri
Mark Zangrilli
Ira Zaslow
Kenneth Albert Zelman
Abraham J. Zelmanowitz
Martin Morales Zempoaltecatl
Zhe Zeng
Marc Scott Zeplin
Jie Yao Justin Zhao
Ivelin Ziminski
Michael Joseph Zinzi
Charles A. Zion
Julie Lynne Zipper
Salvatore Zisa
Prokopios Paul Zois
Joseph J. Zuccala
Andrew S. Zucker
Igor Zukelman

American Airlines Flight 11 Victims

Anna Allison
David Lawrence Angell
Lynn Edwards Angell

Seima Aoyama
Barbara Jean Arestegui
Myra Joy Aronson
Christine Barbuto
Carolyn Beug
Kelly Ann Booms
Carol Marie Bouchard
Robin Lynne Kaplan
Neilie Anne Heffernan Casey
Jeffrey Dwayne Collman
Jeffrey W. Coombs
Tara Kathleen Creamer
Thelma Cuccinello
Patrick Currivan
Brian Paul Dale
David Dimeglio
Donald Americo Ditullio
Alberto Dominguez
Paige Marie Farley-Hackel
Alexander Milan Filipov
Carol Ann Flyzik
Paul J. Friedman
Karleton D.B. Fyfe
Peter Alan Gay
Linda M. George
Edmund Glazer
Lisa Reinhart Gordenstein
Andrew Peter Charles Curry Green
Peter Paul Hashem
Robert Jay Hayes
Edward R. Hennessy, Jr.
John A. Hofer
Cora Hidalgo Holland
John Nicholas Humber, Jr.
Waleed Joseph Iskandar
John Charles Jenkins
Charles Edward Jones
Barbara A. Keating
David P. Kovalcin
Judith Camilla Larocque
Natalie Janis Lasden
Daniel John Lee
Daniel M. Lewin
Sara Elizabeth Low
Susan A. Mackay
Karen Ann Martin
Thomas F. McGuinness, Jr.
Christopher D. Mello
Jeffrey Peter Mladenik
Carlos Alberto Montoya
Antonio Jesus Montoya Valdes
Laura Lee Morabito
Mildred Naiman
Laurie Ann Neira
Renee Lucille Newell
Kathleen Ann Nicosia
Jacqueline June Norton
Robert Grant Norton
John Ogonowski
Betty Ann Ong
Jane M. Orth

Thomas Nicholas Pecorelli
Berinthia B. Perkins
Sonia M. Puopolo
David E. Retik
Jean Destrehan Roger
Philip Martin Rosenzweig
Richard Barry Ross
Jessica Leigh Sachs
Rahma Salie
Heather Lee Smith
Dianne Bullis Snyder
Douglas Joel Stone
Xavier Suarez
Madeline Amy Sweeney
Michael Theodoridis
James Anthony Trentini
Mary Barbara Trentini
Pendyala Vamsikrishna
Mary Alice Wahlstrom
Kenneth Waldie
John Joseph Wenckus
Candace Lee Williams
Christopher Rudolph Zarba, Jr.

United Airlines Flight 175 Victims

Alona Abraham
Garnet Edward Bailey
Mark Lawrence Bavis
Graham Andrew Berkeley
Touri Bolourchi
Klaus Bothe
Daniel Raymond Brandhorst
David Reed Gamboa Brandhorst
John Brett Cahill
Christoffer Mikael Carstanjen
John J. Corcoran III
Dorothy Alma de Araujo
Ana Gloria Pocasangre Debarrera
Robert John Fangman
Lisa Anne Frost
Ronald Gamboa
Lynn Catherine Goodchild
Peter M. Goodrich
Douglas Alan Gowell
Francis Edward Grogan
Carl Max Hammond, Jr.
Christine Lee Hanson
Peter Burton Hanson
Susan Kim Hanson
Gerald Francis Hardacre
Eric Hartono
James Edward Hayden
Herbert Wilson Homer
Michael Robert Horrocks
Robert Adrien Jalbert
Amy N. Jarret
Ralph Kershaw
Heinrich Kimmig
Amy R. King
Brian Kinney

Kathryn L. LaBorie
Robert G. Leblanc
Maclovio Lopez, Jr.
Marianne Macfarlane
Alfred Gilles Marchand
Louis Mariani
Juliana McCourt
Ruth Magdaline McCourt
Wolfgang Peter Menzel
Shawn M. Nassaney
Marie Pappalardo
Patrick J. Quigley IV
Frederick Charles Rimmele III
James Roux
Jesus Sanchez
Victor J. Saracini
Mary Kathleen Shearer
Robert M. Shearer
Jane Louise Simpkin
Brian David Sweeney
Michael C. Tarrou
Alicia N. Titus
Timothy Ray Ward
William Michael Weems

Pentagon Victims

USA - United Stated Army

USN - United States Navy

SPC Craig S. Amundson, USA
YN3 Melissa Rose Barnes, USN
MSG Max J. Beilke, Retired
IT2 Kris Romeo Bishundat, USN
Carrie R. Blagburn
COL Canfield D. Boone, ARNG
Donna M. Bowen
Allen P. Boyle
ET3 Christopher L. Burford, USN
ET3 Daniel M. Caballero, USN
SFC Jose O. Calderon-Olmedo, USA
Angelene C. Carter
Sharon A. Carver
SFC John J. Chada, USA, Retired
Rosa Maria Chapa
Julian T. Cooper
LCDR Eric A. Cranford, USN
Ada M. Davis
CAPT Gerald F. DeConto, USN
LTC Jerry D. Dickerson, USA
IT1 Johnnie Doctor, Jr., USN
CAPT Robert E. Dolan, Jr., USN
CDR William H. Donovan, USN
CDR Patrick Dunn, USN
AG1 Edward T. Earhart, USN
LCDR Robert R. Elseth, USNR
SK3 Jamie L. Fallon, USN
Amelia V. Fields
Gerald P. Fisher
AG2 Matthew M. Flocco, USN
Sandra N. Foster

CAPT Lawrence D. Getzfred, USN
Cortez Ghee
Brenda C. Gibson
COL Ronald F. Golinski, USA, Retired
Diane Hale-McKinzy
Carolyn B. Halmon
Sheila M.S. Hein
ET1 Ronald J. Hemenway, USN
MAJ Wallace Cole Hogan, Jr., USA
SSG Jimmie I. Holley, USA, Retired
Angela M. Houtz
Brady Kay Howell
Peggie M. Hurt
LTC Stephen N. Hyland, Jr., USA
Lt Col Robert J. Hymel, USAF, Retired
SGM Lacey B. Ivory, USA
LTC Dennis M. Johnson, USA
Judith L. Jones
Brenda Kegler
LT Michael S. Lamana, USN
David W. Laychak
Samantha L. Lightbourn-Allen
MAJ Stephen V. Long, USA
James T. Lynch, Jr.
Terence M. Lynch
OS2 Nehamon Lyons IV, USN
Shelley A. Marshall
Teresa M. Martin
Ada L. Mason-Acker
LTC Dean E. Mattson, USA
LTG Timothy J. Maude, USA
Robert J. Maxwell
Molly L. McKenzie
Patricia E. Mickley
MAJ Ronald D. Milam, USA
Gerard P. Moran, Jr.
Odessa V. Morris
ET1 Brian A. Moss, USN
Teddington H. Moy
LCDR Patrick J. Murphy, USNR
Khang Ngoc Nguyen
DM2 Michael A. Noeth, USN
Ruben S. Ornedo
Diana B. Padro
LT Jonas M. Panik, USNR
MAJ Clifford L. Patterson, Jr., USA
LT Darin H. Pontell, USNR
Scott Powell
CAPT Jack D. Punches, USN, Retired
AW1 Joseph J. Pycior, Jr., USN
Deborah A. Ramsaur
Rhonda Sue Rasmussen
IT1 Marsha D. Ratchford, USN
Martha M. Reszke
Cecelia E. (Lawson) Richard
Edward V. Rowenhorst
Judy Rowlett
SGM Robert E. Russell, USA, Retired
CW4 William R. Ruth, ARNG
Charles E. Sabin, Sr.
Marjorie C. Salamone

COL David M. Scales, USA
CDR Robert A. Schlegel, USN
Janice M. Scott
LTC Michael L. Selves, USA, Retired
Marian H. Serva
CDR Dan F. Shanower, USN
Antionette M. Sherman
Diane M. Simmons
Cheryle D. Sincock
ITC Gregg H. Smallwood, USN
LTC Gary F. Smith, USA, Retired
Patricia J. Statz
Edna L. Stephens
SGM Larry L. Strickland, USA
LTC Kip P. Taylor, USA
Sandra C. Taylor
LTC Karl W. Teepe, USA, Retired
SGT Tamara C. Thurman, USA
LCDR Otis V. Tolbert, USN
SSG Willie Q. Troy, USA, Retired
LCDR Ronald J. Vauk, USNR
LTC Karen J. Wagner, USA
Meta L. (Fuller) Waller
SPC Chin Sun Pak Wells, USA
SSG Maudlyn A. White, USA
Sandra L. White
Ernest M. Willcher
LCDR David L. Williams, USN
MAJ Dwayne Williams, USA
RMC Marvin Roger Woods, USN, Retired
IT2 Kevin W. Yokum, USN
ITC Donald M. Young, USN
Edmond G. Young, Jr.
Lisa L. Young

American Airlines Flight 77 Victims

Paul W. Ambrose
Yeneneh Betru
Mary Jane Booth
Bernard C. Brown, II
CAPT Charles F. Burlingame III, USNR, Retired
Suzanne M. Calley
William E. Caswell
David M. Charlebois
Sarah M. Clark

Asia S. Cottom
James D. Debeuneure
Rodney Dickens
Eddie A. Dillard
LCDR Charles A. Droz III, USN, Retired
Barbara G. Edwards
Charles S. Falkenberg
Dana Falkenberg
Zoe Falkenberg
J. Joseph Ferguson
Darlene E. Flagg
RADM Wilson F. Flagg, USNR, Retired
1stLt Richard P. Gabriel, USMC, Retired
Ian J. Gray
Stanley R. Hall
Michele M. Heidenberger
Bryan C. Jack
Steven D. Jacoby
Ann C. Judge
Chandler R. Keller
Yvonne E. Kennedy
Norma Cruz Khan
Karen Ann Kincaid
Dong Chul Lee
Jennifer Lewis
Kenneth E. Lewis
Renee A. May
Dora Marie Menchaca
Christopher C. Newton
Barbara K. Olson
Ruben S. Ornedo
Robert Penninger
Robert R. Ploger III
Zandra F. Ploger
Lisa J. Raines
Todd H. Reuben
John P. Sammartino
George W. Simmons
Donald D. Simmons
Mari-Rae Sopper
Robert Speisman
Norma Lang Steuerle
Hilda E. Taylor
Leonard E. Taylor
Sandra D. Teague
Leslie A. Whittington
CAPT John D. Yamnicky, Sr., USN, Retired

Vicki Yancey
Shuyin Yang
Yuguag Zheng

United Airlines Flight 93 Victims

Christian Adams
Lorraine G. Bay
Todd Beamer
Alan Beaven
Mark K. Bingham
Deora Frances Bodley
Sandra W. Bradshaw
Marion Britton
Thomas E. Burnett Jr.
William Cashman
Georgine Rose Corrigan
Patricia Cushing
Jason Dahl
Joseph Deluca
Patrick Driscoll
Edward Porter Felt
Jane C. Folger
Colleen Fraser
Andrew Garcia
Jeremy Glick
Lauren Grandcolas
Wanda A. Green
Donald F. Greene
Linda Gronlund
Richard Guadagno
Leroy Homer, Jr.
Toshiya Kuge
CeeCee Lyles
Hilda Marcin
Waleska Martinez
Nicole Miller
Louis J. Nacke, II
Donald Arthur Peterson
Jean Hoadley Peterson
Mark Rothenberg
Christine Snyder
John Talignani
Honor Elizabeth Wainio
Deborah Ann Jacobs Welsh
Kristin Gould White

Sources

The 9/11 Commission Report, published 2004

Collier's Encyclopedia Volume 1, pp. 184-191 Copyright 1991 Macmillan Educational Company

The Columbia Encyclopedia as accessed through Yahoo.com

New World Encyclopedia www.newworldencyclopedia.org/entry/Info:Main_Page

Wikipedia www.wikipedia.org

The National September 11 Memorial www.911memorial.org/

Flight 93 National Memorial www.nps.gov/flni/index.htm

Flight 93 National Memorial Campaign (funding) www.honorflight93.org/

The Pentagon September 11 Memorial http://pentagonmemorial.org/

Massachusetts Port Authority 9/11 Memorial website www.massport.com/logan-airport/inside-airport/911%20Memorial/911Memorial.aspx

Fox News September 11 victim's list www.foxnews.com/story/0,2933,62151,00.html

Illustrations

Photo Credits

Smoking Towers, p. 13. The National September 11 Memorial Website

Damaged Pentagon, p. 14. National 9/11 Pentagon Memorial Website

Crash at Shanksville, p. 14. Flight 93 National Memorial Website

The U.S. Capitol, p. 14. U.S. government photo.

Ayatollah Khomeini, p. 17. conservapedia.com

Iran Embassy Storming, p. 17. conservapedia.com

Tomahawk Launch, p. 19. U.S. Navy photo by Lt.j.g. Monika Hess/Released

Rescue at the Pentagon, p. 20. U.S. Air Force photo by Staff Sgt. Gary Coppage

Tribute in Light, p. 22. U.S. Air Force photo/Denise Gould

USAF Memorial, p. 58. Flickr user kathleensulli www.flickr.com/photos/16066043@N08

Pentagon Memorial at Night, pp. 47, 56. Tony Park, Silver Spring, MD. www.flickr.com/photos/79493961@N00/

Flight 93 National Memorial webcam, p. 65. www.honorflight93.org/

Boston Logan International Airport 9/11 Memorial at Night, p. 77. Massachusetts Port Authority photo.

INDEX

9/11 Commission Report 23
Abdul Aziz al Omari 20
Afghanistan 17, 18, 19, 20, 22
Ahmad al Haznawi 21
Ahmed al Ghamdi 20
Ahmed al Nami 21
al Qaeda 16, 19, 20, 23
America 9
American Airlines Flight 11 .... 20, 21, 80
American Airlines Flight 77 .... 20, 21
Ayatollah Ruhollah Khomeini 17
Ayman al Zawahiri 19
Boston 15, 20, 21, 79, 80
Boston Logan airport 15
Congress 14, 22
Dar es Salaam, Tanzania 19
Dhahran 19
Dulles International Airport 20, 21
Earle Naval Weapons Station 13
fatwa 19
Fayez Banihammad 20
Federal Aviation Administration 13
Flight 77 46
Frank Lloyd Wright 68
Hamza al Ghamdi 20
Hani Hanjour 20
Hezbollah 17
Homeland Security 22
hostage crisis 17
Iran 17, 18, 110
Iran-Iraq War 18
Iraq 17, 18, 22
Islamic extremists 16
Khalid al Mihdhar 20
Khalid Sheik Mohammed 16
Khalid Sheikh Mohammed 23
Khobar Towers 19
Kurds 17
Kuwait 18, 22
Lebanon 18
Libya 18
Lockerbie, Scotland 18
Majed Moqed 20
Marines 17
Marwan al Shehhi 20
memorial 9
memorials 9
Mohammed Atta 20
Mohammed Reza Pahlavi 17
Mohand al Shehri 20
Mujahideen 17
Nairobi, Kenya 19
National September 11 Memorial 9
Nawaf al Hazmi 20
New Jersey 3, 9, 13, 14, 23
New York City 9, 13, 14, 27, 47
Newark International Airport 21
Northern Alliance 22
Oklahoma City, Oklahoma 18
Osama bin Ladin 13, 16, 17, 18, 20, 23
Pakistan 16, 23
Pan Am 18
Patriot Act 22
Pentagon .13, 14, 15, 20, 21, 23, 28, 45, 46, 47, 110
Planes Operation 20
President Bush 13, 14, 21, 22
President Carter 17
President Clinton 18
President George H.W. Bush 18
President Reagan 17, 18
President Saddam Hussein 17, 22, 23
Riyadh 18
Saeed al Ghamdi 21

Salem al Hazmi 20
Satam al Suqami 20
Saudi Arabia 18, 19
September 11, 2001 ... 5, 13, 14, 16, 17, 20, 28, 47, 82, 91
Shanksville, Pennsylvania 14, 21, 47, 66, 67
Somalia 18
Soviet Union 17, 18
Sudan 19
Taliban 19, 20, 22
terrorist 9
terrorists 9
Terry Nicohls 18
The 9/11 Commission Report 17, 109
Timothy Mcveigh 18
U.S. embassy 17, 19
United Airlines Flight 175 .... 20, 21, 80
United Airlines Flight 93 21
United Flight 93 .... 14, 20, 67
United States 4, 9, 13, 14, 16, 17, 18, 20, 21
USS Cole 20
victims 9
Wail al Shehri 20
Waleed al Shehri 20
Washington D.C. 14, 20
White House 14, 20, 21
World Trade Center .. 13, 14, 15, 18, 20, 21, 23, 27, 28, 47, 80
WTC 22, 29, 44
Yemen 20
Ziad Jarrah 21

About the Authors

Brian Holmes graduated from Northern Michigan University in the beautiful Upper Peninsula of Michigan with a Bachelor of Science degree in English Creative Writing, with minors in Philosophy and Conservation. That summer he began working in the publishing industry by writing local sports for a penny shopper newspaper, and was paid in pennies for his time. Mr. Holmes has continued to work in publishing for many years, as a proofreader, copy editor, editor, and educational writer.

Brian's other publishing credits include *New Jersey 9/11 Memorials: A Photographic Guide*, *The Devil's Assassin* (a fiction thriller), *What Are You Crying About: Defeating Grief for Christians*, *Energy: The Fuel of Civilization*, and *The Chipmunks' New Neighbors* (children's book). Brian is an avid amateur photographer, history buff, political observer, and blogger.

Min Xie is from the city of Guangzhou in Guangdong province, China and has resided in the U.S. since 2009. She is an artist, having taken classes at Hua Nan Art College. Xie is also adept at photography and photoediting and has more than ten years experience in consumer photo production and sales. Holmes and Xie have been married since 11/11/11 and live in New Jersey.

For more information go to www.nj911memorials.com, or e-mail editor@holmeshousepress.com

Made in the USA
Middletown, DE
13 January 2019